Pocket
NEW ORLEANS

TOP SIGHTS • LOCAL LIFE • MADE EASY

Adam Karlin

In This Book

QuickStart Guide

Your keys to under-standing the city – we help you decide what to do and how to do it

Need to Know
Tips for a smooth trip

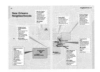

Neighborhoods
What's where

Explore New Orleans

The best things to see and do, neighborhood by neighborhood

Top Sights
Make the most of your visit

Local Life
The insider's city

The Best of New Orleans

The city's highlights in handy lists to help you plan

Best Walks
See the city on foot

New Orleans' Best...
The best experiences

Survival Guide

Tips and tricks for a seamless, hassle-free city experience

Getting Around
Travel like a local

Essential Information
Including where to stay

Our selection of the city's best places to eat, drink and experience:

◉ **Sights**

✖ **Eating**

🚇 **Drinking**

✪ **Entertainment**

🔒 **Shopping**

These symbols give you the vital information for each listing:

☐ Telephone Numbers	⊞ Family-Friendly
☺ Opening Hours	☺ Pet-Friendly
P Parking	☐ Bus
⊖ Nonsmoking	⚓ Ferry
@ Internet Access	M Metro
☎ Wi-Fi Access	S Subway
✔ Vegetarian Selection	☐ Tram
☐ English-Language Menu	☐ Train

Find each listing quickly on maps for each neighborhood:

Bar Hemingway

16 🚇 Map p233, B2

Legend has it that Hemi self, wielding a machine ...rate this timber-pan ...ered bar during ...showpiece is a ...en by Papa ar town. Dress ...s.com; Hôtel Rit ☺ 6.30pm-2a

6 ◉ Plac V...

Lonely Planet's New Orleans

Lonely Planet Pocket Guides are designed to get you straight to the heart of the city.

Inside you'll find all the must-see sights, plus tips to make your visit to each one really memorable. We've split the city into easy-to-navigate neighborhoods and provided clear maps so you'll find your way around with ease. Our expert authors have searched out the best of the city: walks, food, nightlife and shopping, to name a few. Because you want to explore, our 'Local Life' pages will take you to some of the most exciting areas to experience the real New Orleans.

And of course you'll find all the practical tips you need for a smooth trip: itineraries for short visits, how to get around, and how much to tip the guy who serves you a drink at the end of a long day's exploration.

It's your guarantee of a really great experience.

Our Promise

You can trust our travel information because Lonely Planet authors visit the places we write about, each and every edition. We never accept freebies for positive coverage, so you can rely on us to tell it like it is.

QuickStart Guide 7

New Orleans Top Sights.......8

New Orleans Local Life.......12

New Orleans
Day Planner.......14

Need to Know.......16

New Orleans
Neighborhoods.......18

Explore New Orleans 21

22 French Quarter

44 Faubourg Marigny & Bywater

56 CBD & Warehouse District

72 Garden & Lower Garden Districts

86 Uptown & Audubon

104 Mid-City & Bayou St John

116 Tremé

Worth a Trip:

Exploring the Riverbend.......**102**

The Best of New Orleans 127

New Orleans' Best Walks

Balconies & Courtyards 128
Garden District Stroll 130

New Orleans' Best...

Eating 132
Live Music 134
Shopping 136
Bars & Clubs 137
Gay & Lesbian 138
For Kids 139
Architecture 140
Tours 142
Festivals 143
Parks & Gardens 144
Museums 145
Theater 146

Survival Guide 147

Before You Go 148
Arriving in New Orleans ... 149
Getting Around 150
Essential Information 151

QuickStart Guide

New Orleans Top Sights 8

New Orleans Local Life 12

New Orleans Day Planner 14

Need to Know 16

New Orleans Neighborhoods 18

Welcome to New Orleans

New Orleans is an unapologetic, never-ending feast. It's a city that combines the architecture of centuries past, the arts of Europe, the heritage of the Caribbean and the energy of the USA into something unique and special. People here don't consider being a 'hedonist' an insult, because living for music, food and fun is seen as leading a balanced lifestyle.

Celebrating Mardi Gras (p97), Bourbon St
RAY LASKOWITZ/GETTY IMAGES ©

New Orleans Top Sights

Jackson Square (p28)

This is the city's public green space, where its citizens and visitors come to relax, listen to music, perform, people-watch, shop, stroll and generally soak up the city.

KYLIE MCLAUGHLIN/GETTY IMAGES ©

Cabildo (p26)

The history of Louisiana, a state formed from a unique confluence of Caribbean, African, American and European demographics, is the focus of this excellent museum, itself an important historical structure.

Royal Street (p24)

The carnival of human creativity that is the French Quarter unfolds in a series of art galleries, street performances, classical architecture and wrought-iron balconies on Royal St.

National WWII Museum (p58)

American involvement in the largest war in human history is explored from both a soldier's-eye view and a general's sweeping perspective via an enormous collection of largely interactive exhibits.

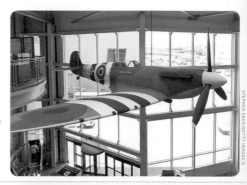

STEPHEN SAKS/GETTY IMAGES ©

Ogden Museum of Southern Art (p60)

The distinctive culture and history of the American South has often found its voice via art. That aesthetic expression, both historical and contemporary, is the focus of this excellent museum.

RICHARD CUMMINS/GETTY IMAGES ©

Lafayette Cemetery No 1 (p74)

The carved stone angels, eruptions of creeping vines and imposing mausoleums of this cemetery are like a perfect physical distillation of the Southern Gothic aesthetic.

ROB PILECKIS/GETTY IMAGES ©

St Charles Avenue Streetcar (p88)

This mobile piece of urban transportation history clatters through the bucolic streets of Uptown, bearing passengers along picturesque St Charles Ave, a street as important to American architecture as Frank Lloyd Wright.

Audubon Zoological Gardens (p90)

Home to lazy gators basking in a green swamp, Audubon Zoo not only introduces visitors to the wildlife of the world, but re-creates the wilderness of Louisiana.

City Park (p106)

Long lines of live oaks, scale models of the city, Greek columns, a sculpture garden and a singing tree: it's easy to fall in love with New Orleans' largest park. Pictured (left) is a 1910 Gates Pottery terracotta portico urn from the park's New Orleans Museum of Art (NOMA; p110).

New Orleans Local Life

Insider tips to help you find the real city

New Orleans is friendly to its visitors, but far more rewarding to those who learn its little secrets and find the local hangouts that are integral to this fascinating city's cultural fabric.

A Night of Jazz & Live Music (p46)

▶ Music clubs
▶ Neighborhood dive bars

Faubourg Marigny has a fantastic concentration of venues where the sounds range from classic jazz to contemporary dance. Experience it all on this journey through clubs that play out the backbeat of the city's soul.

Gallery-Hopping in the Arts District (p62)

▶ Long lines of art galleries
▶ Artisan souvenir shopping

Many cities have gallery districts and arts walks, but few have the caliber of talent and capacity for celebration to match New Orleans. Arts nights in this city are special; here's how we approach the evening.

Shopping on Magazine Street (p73)

▶ Independent boutiques
▶ Designer goods and vintage shops

Magazine St stretches out in a long upturned smile of independent shops. This enormous commercial corridor features goods ranging from curated antiques to art supplies including galleries, jewelry designers and bespoke tailors.

Audubon Park & Around (p92)

▶ Tulane exhibitions
▶ Lush lawns for lounging

Join the beautiful people and students from Tulane and Loyola as they jog, jump, picnic and otherwise experience a beautiful piece of landscaping that anchors Uptown. You can also explore some of Tulane University's enormous cultural resources.

Exploring the Riverbend (p102)

▶ Student-oriented shops
▶ Fantastic affordable dining

The Riverbend is one of the more student-heavy neighborhoods in the city. It's a cosmopolitan area as well, with international ethnic dining options balanced by a fantastic selection of nightlife.

Audubon Park (p92)

Magazine Street (p73)

Other great places to experience the city like a local:

Faulkner House Books (p43)

Fair Grinds (p113)

Clouet Gardens (p52)

Central Grocery (p40)

Southern Food & Beverage Museum (p82)

Café du Monde (p39)

Mardi Gras World (p69)

Angelo Brocato (p112)

Boot (p99)

New Orleans Day Planner

Day One

New Orleans is well known for its cafe culture, so you may as well start the day at one of its coziest coffee houses with a croissant and café au lait at **Croissant D'Or** (p37). Afterwards, the French Quarter is at your fingertips. Head to **Jackson Square** (p28) and have a wander around the **Cabildo** (p26), which provides an excellent introduction to the history of New Orleans and Louisiana.

Have lunch at **SoBou** (p36), then wander up Royal St, all while perusing galleries and antique shops. At some point, you may want to head to the **Riverfront** (p32) and take in views of the Mississippi. Take a walk through the **French Market** (p32), and then head to the **Old US Mint** (p32) for a free concert.

Eat dinner at grungy, unapologetically unhealthy **Coop's** (p36) – the service is kind of surly, but the food is divine. The Cajun cuisine here will make you want to take a 12-hour nap, but the night isn't over yet. Walk up to **Frenchmen Street** (p49) and take in the live music the city is famous for.

Day Two

On your second day in town, head to the Garden District and Uptown. The best way around, if you're taking your time, is via the **St Charles Avenue Streetcar** (p88). Take it into the Garden District and be sure to stop in for breakfast at **Surrey's Juice Bar** (p81). Wander along Magazine St and get some shopping in amid a sea of independent boutiques.

For lunch, you can't go wrong with one of the deli sandwiches at **Stein's** (p82). Don't worry, there will be time for po'boys in the future. For now, visit **Lafayette Cemetery No 1** (p74) and soak up some slightly creepy Southern Gothic. Head back towards the streetcar, and consider a drink at the **Columns Hotel** (p100).

Now, as evening sets in, you're in the area known as Uptown. Traditionally, this is one of the wealthier parts of town, and there's a good spread of restaurants. You can try an oyster, bacon and cheese po'boy at **Mahony's Po-Boy Shop** (p96), which offers (besides the eponymous item) truly innovative takes on iconic New Orleans cuisine. Finish the day with a drink in the courtyard at **St Joe's** (p99).

Short on time?
We've arranged New Orleans' must-sees into these day-by-day itineraries to make sure you see the very best of the city in the time you have available.

Day Three

Grab breakfast at **Lil' Dizzy's** (p123) and head into the Tremé, the oldest African American neighborhood in the country. You may want to ride a bicycle, as the area is very bike friendly. Don't miss **St Augustine's Church** (p120) or the **Backstreet Cultural Museum** (p120), both of which provide excellent insight into the city's African American history and folkways.

You may have to wait in line, but it's worth it for the fried chicken at **Willie Mae's** (p123); we don't know what the folk in the kitchen do with those birds, but they're doing it right. Continue up Esplanade Ave and gawk at all the gorgeous Creole mansions until you reach **City Park** (p106). You can easily fill a day here wandering the grounds and visiting the **New Orleans Museum of Art** (p110) and **Sydney & Walda Besthoff Sculpture Garden** (p110).

Try to catch the sunset over Bayou St John, the city's own inland waterfront. When night falls, enjoy a romantic dinner at **Café Degas** (p112), which sits on a particularly atmospheric intersection. Later, go grab drinks at **Pal's** (p114) or **Twelve Mile Limit** (p113), two of the finest neighborhood bars in the city.

Day Four

Start your day in the Warehouse District and explore around the **Ogden Museum of Southern Art** (p60) and the **National WWII Museum** (p58) – if you've only got time for one, pick your passion between art and history. Then grab a cab or ride a bicycle to Press St.

After you cross the train tracks at Press St, you're in the Bywater. Have lunch at **Pizza Delicious** (p50), then browse the excellent collection of music at **Euclid Records** (p55). Afterwards, walk off that pizza in the **Crescent Park** (p49), a waterfront green space that affords fantastic views of the Mississippi River. There's a great collection of candy-colored houses scattered throughout this neighborhood.

Have dinner at **Bacchanal** (p50), a restaurant that combines a sweet outdoor garden with an enormous selection of cheese, wine and other things that make life worth living. After dinner, start making your way back into the Marigny towards the French Quarter. Stop into **Mimi's in the Marigny** (p52) to see if any music is playing, or to just enjoy a drink and some small-plate food.

Need to Know

**For more information,
see Survival Guide (p147)**

Currency
US dollars ($)

Language
English

Visas
Required for most foreign visitors unless
eligible for the Visa Waiver Program.

Money
ATMs widely available. Credit cards
accepted in all accommodations and many,
but not all, restaurants.

Cell Phones
Local SIM cards can be used in European
and Australian phones. Other phones must
be set to roaming.

Time
Central Time (GMT/UTC minus six hours)

Plugs & Adaptors
Plugs have two straight pins and one hole.
Visitors will have to bring adaptors.
Voltage is 120V.

Tipping
Mandatory. Tip servers 18%, or 20% for good
service. Bartenders get $1 per round,
or more if you order several drinks or
complex cocktails.

① Before You Go

Your Daily Budget

Budget less than $100
- ▶ Dorm bed $30
- ▶ Self-catering or cheap takeout $10
- ▶ Rent a bicycle ($30) or use streetcars ($3)

Midrange $100–200
- ▶ Guesthouse or B&B room $100–120
- ▶ Neighborhood restaurant for two $50–70
- ▶ Bicycle rental or split taxi fares $30

Top end more than $200
- ▶ Fine dining for two including wine $150
- ▶ Four-star double hotel room from $200
- ▶ Taxis or car rental $70

Useful Websites

Gambit (www.bestofneworleans.com) Arts
and entertainment listings.

New Orleans Online (www.neworleans
online.com) Official tourism website.

New Orleans CVB (www.neworleanscvb.com)
Convention Center & Visitor Bureau.

WWOZ radio (www.wwoz.org) Firm finger on
the cultural pulse.

Lonely Planet (www.lonelyplanet.com/usa/
new-orleans) Your trusted traveler website.

Advance Planning

Three months before Check what festivals
are on; book hotel rooms if arriving during
Mardi Gras or Jazz Fest.

One month before Organize car rental.
Book at high-end restaurants you don't
want to miss.

One week before Check the *Gambit* and
New Orleans Online for live music on
during your visit.

② Arriving in New Orleans

Most travelers enter via Louis Armstrong New Orleans International Airport (MSY; www.flymsy.com). The remainder arrive via bus or train into the Amtrak and Greyhound stations, which are adjacent to each other, or drive in via the I-10 or US 90.

✈ From Louis Armstrong Airport

Destination	Best Transportation
French Quarter	Taxi
CBD & Warehouse District	Shuttle
Faubourg Marigny & Bywater	Taxi
Garden District	Taxi
Uptown	Taxi
Mid-City	E-2 bus
Tremé	Taxi

From Amtrak & Greyhound

Taxis are easily available from the Amtrak and Greyhound terminal and are the easiest option to get to your chosen neighborhood. Taxis cost around $10 to the French Quarter or CBD, and a little more to go further afield.

③ Getting Around

Flat New Orleans lacks both elevation and good infrastructure. By far the easiest way around is by car or bicycle. Public transportation is lacking, but you can find schedules online at www.norta.com. The streetcar is slow, but atmospheric for exploring the Garden District and Uptown.

🚗 Car

The easiest way to access outer neighborhoods such as Mid-City. Parking is problematic in the French Quarter and CBD, but elsewhere street parking isn't too hard to find.

🚲 Bicycle

Flat New Orleans is easy to cycle across – you can cross the entire city in 45 minutes.

🚋 Streetcar

Service on the charming streetcars is limited. One-way fares cost $1.25, and multi-trip passes are available.

🚌 Bus

Bus services are OK, but try not to time your trip around them. Fares won't run more than $2.

Walk

If you're just exploring within the French Quarter, the Marigny and Bywater and even the CBD your feet will serve you fine.

New Orleans Neighborhoods

Mid-City & Bayou St John (p104)

This gorgeous residential area abuts lovely City Park and strikes the golden mean between lush greenery and urban character.

⊙ Top Sights

City Park

Garden & Lower Garden Districts (p72)

Enormous live oak trees shade an affluent neighborhood intersected by parade routes, countless cafes and student bars.

⊙ Top Sights

Lafayette Cemetery No 1

Uptown & Audubon (p86)

Student scene, mansions, high-end shopping and haute cuisine combine in one of New Orleans' most beautiful neighborhoods.

⊙ Top Sights

St Charles Avenue Streetcar

Audubon Zoological Gardens

⊙ *City Park*

St Charles Avenue Streetcar
⊙

Audubon
⊙ *Zoological Gardens*

Tremé (p116)
The oldest African American neighborhood in the country has its finger firmly on the cultural pulse of the city.

Faubourg Marigny & Bywater (p44)
These two bohemian neighborhoods represent the artsy, gentrified edge of the city. Innovative bars, food and unbeatable live music abound.

Cabildo

Jackson Square

Royal Street

Ogden Museum of Southern Art

National WWII Museum

French Quarter (p22)
A tight concentration of historical buildings that contains an adult theme park centered on food, drink and music.

⊙ Top Sights

Royal Street

Cabildo

Jackson Square

Lafayette Cemetery No 1

CBD & Warehouse District (p56)
The traditional downtown business district, peppered with red-brick, reconstituted warehouses and high-rises.

⊙ Top Sights

National WWII Museum

Ogden Museum of Southern Art

Explore
New Orleans

French Quarter `22`

Faubourg Marigny & Bywater `44`

CBD & Warehouse District `56`

Garden & Lower Garden Districts `72`

Uptown & Audubon `86`

Mid-City & Bayou St John `104`

Tremé `116`

Worth a Trip

Exploring the Riverbend..........................102

St Louis Cathedral (p29), French Quarter
KYLIE MCLAUGHLIN/GETTY IMAGES ©

Explore

French Quarter

The French Quarter is the heart of New Orleans tourism. Away from boozy Bourbon St, you'll find a condensed collection of historical Creole architecture, great museums and some of the city's best dining, drinking and shopping. When you hear trumpet and guitar notes waft past iconic iron balconies, you'll start to feel the magic that has moved generations of poets, dreamers and musicians.

FRANZ MARC FREY/LOOK-FOTO/GETTY® IMAGES ©

The Sights in a Day

☼ Renting a bicycle is a great way to get around; you can cover a lot more ground that way. We recommend starting your day with a pastry and a strong cup of coffee at **Croissant D'Or** (p37). Then head to **Jackson Square** (p28) and lose yourself among the collections of the **Cabildo** (p26); make sure to get your tarot cards read on the square afterwards

☼ Stop for lunch at **SoBou** (p36), then take a walk along the Mississippi River and consider catching a concert at the **Old US Mint** (p32). Now that you're at the 'bottom' of the Quarter, wander into the **French Market** (p32), and then head back towards Canal St while catching some outdoor music and magic along **Royal Street** (p24).

☽ Go shopping for magic spells at **Esoterica Occult Goods** (p43) and get to **Preservation Hall** (p42) early enough to see a show. Now it's time to sample some of the most decadent cuisine in the city. Finish with dinner at **Bayona** (p36) and drinks at **Erin Rose** (p40) or **Tonique** (p39); if you want a tropical cocktail, head to **Latitude 29** (p39).

 Top Sights

Royal Street (p24)

Cabildo (p26)

Jackson Square (p28)

♥ **Best of New Orleans**

Eating
Bayona (p36)

Green Goddess (p39)

Live Music
Preservation Hall (p42)

House of Blues (p42)

Bars & Clubs
Tonique (p39)

French 75 (p40)

Museums
Cabildo (p26)

The Historic New Orleans Collection (p32)

Getting There

🚋 **Streetcar** The Canal and Riverfront streetcars both skirt the edges of the Quarter.

🚌 **Bus** No 91 runs up Rampart St and Esplanade Ave, boundary roads of the Quarter.

🚗 **Car** Parking is a hassle; if you're going to drive here, either be prepared to park in a garage or bring lots of quarters for meters.

Top Sights
Royal Street

With its high-end antique shops, block after block of galleries, and potted ferns hanging from cast-iron balconies, Royal St is the elegant yin to the Quarter's more famous strip – Bourbon St – and its Sodom-and-Gomorrah yang. Head here to engage in culinary and consumer indulgence rather than party-till-unconscious excess. Stroll or bicycle past the patinated, fading grace and beauty of its architecture and get a sense of the fun – with a dash of elegance – that used to be the soul of the Vieux Carré (French Quarter).

◉ Map p30, A7

Musicians, French Quarter

Don't Miss

Pedestrian Performances

The blocks of Royal St between St Ann and St Louis Sts are closed to car traffic during the afternoon. Musicians, performers and other buskers set up shop; you may see some teenage runaways shill for pennies, or accomplished blues musicians jam on their Fenders. Either way, the show is (almost) always entertaining.

Architecture

Few people live on the 13 blocks that constitute the French Quarter stretch of Royal; this wasn't always the way, though, as attested to by rows of wrought-iron balconies and closely packed Creole town houses. Behind many of these buildings are enormous gardens and leafy courtyards, once spaces of escape from the street scene, now often used as dining spaces by restaurants.

Louisiana Supreme Court

At 400 Royal St, you'll encounter the imposing edifice of the Louisiana Supreme Court. This massive beaux-arts building was considered an out-of-scale addition to the Quarter at the time of its construction in 1910. The statue in front is of Edward Douglass White, a senator and former chief justice of the US Supreme Court.

Outdoor Arcade

Blocks of Royal St are dedicated to antique stores and art galleries, making this a sort of elegant outdoor shopping arcade. Well, maybe 'elegant' isn't the right word; there's too much of a New Orleanian embrace of playful chaos. On Dirty Linen night, held in August, art galleries throw open their doors and the wine flows free and plentiful.

☑ Top Tips

▶ The 'pedestrian only' zone doesn't just exclude cars; you can't ride a bicycle around here either.

▶ If you're self-catering, there's a decently stocked Rouse's grocery store at 701 Royal St.

▶ Tip those street performers! Especially if you stay and watch the show.

▶ A pedicab is a good means of getting back to either end of Royal St if it's too hot.

✕ Take a Break

If you're in the mood for innovative takes on Creole cuisine, make sure to stop into the excellent Green Goddess (p39).

Those seeking a caffeine jolt should pop into Spitfire Coffee (p41) for its rocket-fuel espresso.

Top Sights
Cabildo

The former seat of power in colonial Louisiana serves as the gateway for exploring the history of the state, and New Orleans in particular. It's also a magnificent building on its own merits. The Cabildo, a Spanish term for a city council (the original structure was built in 1795 under Spanish rule), leads visitors into airy halls reminiscent of Spanish Colonial design. It's topped with a mansard roof (the narrow, steep-sided roofs commonly found in Europe) added in the French style.

◉ Map p30, C5

☏ 800-568-6968, 504-568-6968

www.louisianastatemuseum. org

701 Chartres St

adult/child under 12yr $6/free

🕑 10am-4:30pm Tue-Sun

Louisiana State Museum, Cabildo

Don't Miss

Slavery & Society

Much of the 3rd floor of the museum is given over to slavery and the troubled history of race in Louisiana. It's a refreshingly honest take on the subject, given New Orleans was once an enormous slave port. Handbills offering rewards for escaped slaves are a troubling reminder of the chattel status once reserved for much of the city's population.

Capitol Views

The magnificent Sala Capitular (Capitol Room), a council room fronted by enormous windows and sweeping views onto Jackson Sq, was the most important room in Louisiana for decades. Civic function and legal action were conducted here; this was the courtroom where *Plessy v Ferguson*, the 1896 case that legalized segregation under the 'separate but equal' clause, was heard.

Peoples of the Parishes

The 1st floor of the museum explores the many ethnic groups and communities that have called south Louisiana home, from the original Native American tribes to waves of immigration ranging from the French to the Spanish, Germans, Americans, Irish, Jews and more. There are some particularly gruesome statistics on the prevalence of disease and its toll on Louisiana.

Reconstruction & Louisiana

American author William Faulkner said, 'The past is never dead. It's not even past.' That quote only begins to hint at the troubled history of patching the wounds of the Civil War in the South. The wing of the Cabildo dedicated to post–Civil War Reconstruction is as even-handed and thorough an attempt at explaining this difficult period as we've seen.

MENZANN/GETTY IMAGES ©

☑ Top Tips

▶ Ask about Friends of the Cabildo walking tours of different New Orleans neighborhoods.

▶ There are great photo opportunities from the Sala Capitular.

▶ Traveling with kids? The museum website has printable scavenger hunts tailored to different age ranges.

▶ The Cabildo is big – give yourself two hours to explore.

✕ Take a Break

Just a short toddle from the Cabildo is Sylvain (p38), a sexy gastropub where you can top off your museum time with a nice cocktail and roast quail.

If you fancy a splurge, the decadent SoBou (p36) serves up some of the most eclectic nouveau New Orleans cuisine in the Quarter.

Top Sights
Jackson Square

Sprinkled with lazing loungers, surrounded by fortune-tellers, sketch artists and traveling performers, and overlooked by cathedrals, offices and shops plucked from a Paris-meets-the-Caribbean fantasy, Jackson Sq is one of America's great town squares. It both anchors the French Quarter and beats out the rhythm of this corner of town. Whatever happens in the Quarter usually begins here. The identical block-long Pontalba Buildings overlook the square, and the near-identical Cabildo and Presbytère structures flank St Louis Cathedral, the square's centerpiece.

👁 Map p30, C5

Decatur & St Peter Sts

St Louis Cathedral, Jackson Square

Don't Miss

St Louis Cathedral

One of the best examples of French architecture in the country is the triple-spired cathedral dedicated to Louis IX, the French king sainted in 1297. It's an innocuous bit of Gallic heritage in the heart of an American city. Besides hosting black, white and Creole congregants, St Louis attracted those who mixed their religious influences, such as voodoo queen Marie Laveau.

Artists & Entertainers

Jackson Sq is ringed by a wrought-iron fence where artists of all types hang their wares; street performers strut their stuff; tarot cards get read; fortunes are divined; and life generally plays out in all of its fascinating diversity. Brass bands break into performance on a pretty regular basis in the center of the square.

The Jackson Statue

In the middle of the park stands the monument to Andrew Jackson – Clark Mills' bronze equestrian statue of the man, unveiled in 1856. The inscription 'The Union Must and Shall be Preserved' was added by General Benjamin Butler, Union military governor of New Orleans during the Civil War, ostensibly to rub it into the occupied city's face.

Pontalba Buildings

The four-story brick apartment buildings that line either side of Jackson Sq were built by the Baroness Pontalba back in the 1840s. The upper, residential floors are supposedly the oldest continuously rented apartments in the country, while the ground floors house the usual rogues' gallery of French Quarter businesses (T-shirts! Hot sauce! Hot sauce and T-shirts!).

☑ Top Tips

▶ If you watch a busker for more than a minute or take their photo, it's bad form not to tip.

▶ Wander around the edge of the square and gawk at art vendors.

▶ You can bring a bicycle into the square, but you can't ride it – the area's pedestrian-only.

✗ Take a Break

Grab a chicory coffee and a beignet from Café du Monde (p39), and enjoy it on the lawn of Jackson Sq rather than inside the crowded cafe.

If you want to taste some Cajun diner food, you can't go wrong at Coop's (p36).

FAUBOURG
MARIGNY

THE
TREMÉ

FRENCH
QUARTER

200 m
0.1 miles

N Rampart St

N Rampart St

Dauphine St

Kerlerec St

Kerlerec St

Esplanade Ave

Kerlerec St

Barracks St

Governor Nicholls St

Ursulines Ave

Bourbon St

Dauphine St

St Philip St

Dumaine St

St Ann St

Orleans Ave

St Peter St

Burgundy St

Henriette Delille St

Tremé St

Maras St

N Villere St

Old US Mint

French Market Pl

N Peters St

Ursulines

Ursulines

Decatur St

Chartres St

Royal St

St Ann St

Madison St

Dumaine

Louis
Armstrong
Park

Municipal
Auditorium

● 4

✕ 16

● 13

✕ 14

6 Gallier House
Museum

8 Beauregard-
Keyes House

12 ●

● 7

9 ●
22 ●

20 ●

Ursuline
Convent

French
Market 2

● 32

Lower Pontalba
Buildings

● 37

36 ●

35 ●

● 34

23 ●

27 ●

● 30 ● 29

28 ●

Pirate's Al

Antoine Al 5 ●
Presbytère

St Ann St

31 ☆

● 19
✕ 15

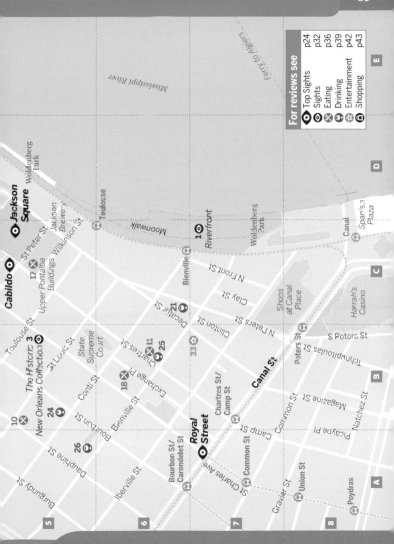

For reviews see

◎	Top Sights	p24
◉	Sights	p32
✗	Eating	p36
◍	Drinking	p39
✿	Entertainment	p42
🛍	Shopping	p43

Sights

Riverfront

PARK

1 Map p30, C7

It's supremely pleasant to stroll up to the Mississippi River as it runs by the Quarter. The entire riverfront area has been landscaped with pedestrian paths, public arts projects and small green spaces such as the **Woldenberg Park**. Sunset is the best time to come up here: couples walk around in love; container ships and ferries ply the water; and all feels bucolic. Nearby is the **Jackson (Jax) Brewery**, a mediocre shopping mall that *does* have free public restrooms. (from Bienville to St Philip St)

✅ Top Tip

Pedicabs

The French Quarter is terrible for driving and parking, and while it can be nice to walk, the distances can be deceptively long (especially if it's hot). The best way around is by bicycle, but if you're uncomfortable riding one, try a New Orleans bicycle taxi/pedicab instead. These three-wheeled contrivances can be found throughout the Quarter, CBD and Marigny. You can flag one down or call the dispatch office; try **New Orleans Bike Taxi** (☑504-891-3441; www.neworleansbiketaxi.com) or **NOLA Pedicabs** (☑504-274-1300; www.nolapedicabs.com). Fares are $1 per passenger, per block traveled.

French Market

MARKET

2 Map p30, D4

Within its shopping arcades of uninspiring souvenirs, it's easy to forget that for centuries this was the great bazaar and pulsing commercial heart for much of New Orleans. Today the French Market is a bit sanitized, a tourist jungle of curios, flea markets and harmless tat that all equals family-friendly fun. (☑504-522-2621; www.frenchmarket.org; 1100 N Peters St; ☺hours vary by vendor)

The Historic New Orleans Collection

MUSEUM

3 Map p30, B5

In several exquisitely restored buildings you'll find thoughtfully curated exhibits with an emphasis on archival materials, such as the original transfer documents of the Louisiana Purchase. Separate home, architecture/courtyard and history tours run at 10am, 11am, 2pm and 3pm, the home one being the most interesting of them. (THNOC; ☑504-523-4662; www.hnoc.org; 533 Royal St; admission free, tours $5; ☺9:30am-4:30pm Tue-Sat, from 10:30am Sun)

Old US Mint

MUSEUM

4 Map p30, E3

The Mint, housed in a blocky Greek-revival structure, is the only building of its kind to have printed both US and Confederate currency. Today it's a museum showcasing rotating exhibits on local history and culture;

French Market

it also contains the Louisiana Historical Center, an archive of manuscripts, microfiche and records related to the state. The Jazz National Historic Park hosts concerts here on weekday afternoons; check in at its office to see who is playing or visit www.musicatthemint.org. (☏800-568-6868, 504-568-6993; www.louisianastatemuseum.org; 400 Esplanade Ave; adult/child $6/5; ⏰10am-4:30pm Tue-Sun)

Presbytère
MUSEUM

5 ◉ Map p30, C4

The lovely Presbytère building, designed in 1791 as a rectory for the St Louis Cathedral, serves as New Orleans' Mardi Gras museum. You'll find there's more to the city's most famous celebration than wanton debauchery – or, at least, discover the many levels of meaning behind the debauchery. There's an encyclopedia's worth of material on the krewes, secret societies, costumes and racial histories of the Mardi Gras tapestry, all intensely illuminating and easy to follow. (☏800-568-6968, 504-568-6968; www.louisianastatemuseum; 751 Chartres St; adult/student $6/5; ⏰10am-4:30pm Tue-Sun; 🚼)

Gallier House Museum
HISTORIC BUILDING

6 ◉ Map p30, D3

Many New Orleans buildings owe their existence, either directly or by design, to James Gallier Sr and Jr, who added Greek-revivalist,

British and American accents to the Quarter's French/Spanish/Creole architectural mélange. In 1857 Gallier Jr began work on this town house, which incorporates all of the above elements. The period furniture is lovely; not so much are the intact slave quarters out back – once you see these, you'll recognize them throughout the French Quarter. (☎504-274-0746; www.hgghh.org; 1132 Royal St; adult/student & senior $12/10; ☺tours hourly 10am-2pm Mon, Tue, Thu & Fri, noon-3pm Sat, by appointment Wed)

Understand
The Big Muddy

The Mississippi River is more than the defining geographical landmark of New Orleans. It is its soul, its center and its reason for being. 'Why was New Orleans built below sea level?' folks ask. First off, only half the city is below sea level, but the reason is that this spot commands the entrance to the most important river in North America. All the trade, conquest and exploration of this continent is wrapped up in the Mississippi and its moods.

Some of our favorite spots for river-watching include numerous benches along the levee opposite Jackson Sq and the Moon Walk, a boardwalk built by and named for former mayor Moon Landrieu.

Ursuline Convent   HISTORIC BUILDING

7 ◉ Map p30, D3

One of the few surviving French Colonial buildings in New Orleans, this lovely convent is worth a tour for its architectural virtues and its small museum of Catholic bric-a-brac. After a five-month voyage from Rouen, France, 12 Ursuline nuns arrived in New Orleans in 1727. The Ursuline had a missionary bent, but achieved their goals through advancing the literacy rate of women of all races and social levels; their school admitted French, Native American and African American girls. (☎504-529-3040; www. stlouiscathedral.org; 1112 Chartres St; adult/ student/senior $5/3/4; ☺10am-4pm Mon-Sat)

Beauregard-Keyes House   HISTORIC BUILDING

8 ◉ Map p30, D3

This 1826 Greek-revival house is named for its two most famous former inhabitants. Confederate General Pierre Gustave Toutant Beauregard commanded the artillery battery that fired the first shots at Fort Sumter in Charleston, SC, starting the Civil War. Francis Parkinson Keyes wrote 51 novels, many of which were set in New Orleans – and one, *Madame Castel's Lodger* (1962), set in this house. (☎504-523-7257; www.bkhouse.org; 1113 Chartres St; tours adult/child/student $10/4/9; ☺tours hourly 10am-3pm Mon-Sat)

Understand

Creole Heritage

You'll hear the term 'Creole' thrown around a lot in south Louisiana, and it's important to define the term and give it some context. Generally, 'Creole' refers to people of mixed ancestry in most of the post–French Colonial world. The implication is often that Creole means mixed race, but this isn't necessarily the case in Louisiana – although it can be (bear with us).

Long story short. Louisiana Creole usually refers to the descendants of the original European colonists who settled this area. Because of the shifting political status of the Louisiana colony (French, then Spanish, then French again), those Europeans were most often from France and Spain. Under the Code Noir – the set of laws that governed slavery in the French empire – if a slave owner sired a child with a slave, that child was born free. Thus, an entire segment of mixed-race New Orleanians, and their descendants, also identifies as Creole in the racialized sense of the word.

Anglo (& Other) Influences

After the Louisiana Purchase in 1803, New Orleans was absorbed into the USA. Unsurprisingly, there was tension between the largely protestant Anglo Americans and Catholic Creole New Orleanians. The latter found the former uncouth and boring; the reverse considered Louisianans feckless and indolent, proving tired regional clichés stretch back for centuries.

New Orleans has a habit of digesting its settlers and turning them into its own, though. Successive waves of immigration into New Orleans have layered onto the city's demographic milieu, but the Creole city that originally existed has teased something quintessentially New Orleanian – a commitment to fun, food and music – out of each new slice of the population pie.

Take the Italians, who suffused local foodways with *muffulettas* and musicality with crooners such as Louis Prima. In a similar vein, the Vietnamese have brought both food and a penchant for festivals; the Vietnamese New Year (Tet) is now a major celebration point for New Orleanians of all creeds and colors. Creole implies admixture, and mixing is something this town excels at, even if it doesn't always do so easily.

Eating

Coop's Place
CAJUN **$**

9 Map p30, D3

Coop's is an authentic Cajun dive, but more rocked out. Make no mistake: it's a grotty chaotic place, the servers have attitude and the layout is annoying. But it's worth it for the food: rabbit jambalaya, chicken with shrimp and *tasso* (smoked ham) in a cream sauce. No patrons under 21. (☎504-525-9053; www.coopsplace.net; 1109 Decatur St; mains $8-18; ⊙11am-3am)

Bayona
LOUISIANAN **$$$**

10 Map p30, B5

Bayona is, for our money, the best splurge in the Quarter. It's rich but not overwhelming, classy but unpretentious, innovative without being precocious, and all around just a very fine spot for a meal. The menu changes regularly, but expect fresh fish, fowl and game prepared in a way that comes off as elegant and deeply cozy at the same time. (☎504-525-4455; www.bayona.com; 430 Dauphine St; mains $29-38; ⊙11:30am-1:30pm Wed-Sun, 6-9:30pm Mon-Thu, 5:30-10pm Fri & Sat)

SoBou
MODERN AMERICAN **$$$**

11 Map p30, B6

The name means 'South of Bourbon.' The food? Hard to pin, but uniformly excellent. The chefs play with a concept that mixes Louisiana indulgence with eccentricities: sweet-potato beignets slathered with duck gravy and

---

Understand
Casket Girls & Working Girls

The early Ursuline nuns observed that an unusually high proportion of the Louisiana colony's women worked the world's oldest profession, so they decided to call in marriageable girls from France (generally recruited from orphanages or convents). The girls arrived with clothes packed in coffin-like trunks, and became known as the 'casket girls.' Educated by nuns, the girls were brought up to make proper wives for the French men of New Orleans.

But prostitution never lost its luster. New Orleans' fabled bordellos are one of the earliest foundations upon which the city's reputation as a spot for sin is built. The most famous 'sporting' houses were mansions, reputedly decorated with some of the finest art and furnishings of their era.

Around the turn of the 20th century, city alderman (councillor) Sidney Story wrote an ordinance that moved bordellos out of the city's posh neighborhoods and into the side of the French Quarter that borders the Tremé. Never ones to pass up good irony, New Orleanians dubbed their red-light district 'Storyville' in honor of Sidney.

Beignets and café au lait, Café du Monde (p39)

chicory coffee glaze, and the infamous, decadent foie gras burger. The on-site bar mixes mean drinks, and there are tables with beer taps built in! (☎504-552-4095; www.sobounola.com; 310 Chartres St; mains $24-38; ⊗7am-10pm)

Croissant D'Or Patisserie
BAKERY $

 12 Map p30, D3

On the quieter side of the French Quarter, this spotlessly clean pastry shop is where many locals start their day. Bring a paper, order coffee and a croissant – or a tart, quiche or sandwich topped with béchamel sauce – and bliss out. Check out the tiled sign on the threshold that says 'ladies entrance' – a holdover from earlier days. (☎504-524-4663; www.croissantdornola.com; 617 Ursulines Ave; meals $3-5; ⊗6am-3pm Wed-Mon)

Port of Call
BURGERS $

 13 Map p30, D2

The Port of Call burger is legendary. The meat is unadulterated and, well, meaty, like umami condensed into a patty. Then there's the baked potato on the side, buckling under the weight of sour cream, butter and bacon bits, all served in a 1960s-ish Polynesian tiki-bar setting. Be prepared to wait outside in long lines for a seat (no reservations). (☎504-523-0120; www.portofcallnola.com; 838 Esplanade Ave; mains $7-21; ⊗11am-midnight, to 1am Fri & Sat)

Verti Marte

DELI $

14 Map p30, D2

Sometimes you just wanna wander the Quarter with a tasty sandwich in hand. If that's the case, get to Verti, a reliable deli with a takeout stand that's got a menu as long as a hot New Orleans summer day. Try the 'All That Jazz,' a ridiculous blend of turkey, shrimp, 'wow sauce,' ham, cheese and who knows what else. (504-525-4767; 1201 Royal St; meals $4-9; ⏱24hr)

Mister Gregory's

FRENCH $

15 Map p30, B3

That the French expat community of New Orleans regularly makes its way

Top Tip

Self-Catering in the Quarter

If you're into self-catering, the French Market (p32) may seem like a natural destination, but bear in mind only a vestige of former market activity remains. Largely it has become a pavilion for local food purveyors selling deli sandwiches, po'boys and other foodstuffs; hours vary by vendor, but most spots open around 9am and shut around 6pm. That said, an actual farmers market with fresh produce and meats is open at the French Market on Wednesdays from 2pm to 6pm and Saturdays from 10am to 2pm. There is also a Rouse's grocery store at 701 Royal St (open 6am to 1am).

to Mister Gregory's should tell you something about the quality of this bistro's baguettes and sandwiches. This simple lunch and breakfast spot specializes in deli baguettes, plus does a mean line of *croque*-style sandwiches (ie with melted cheese and béchamel on top), salads and waffles. (504-407-3780; www.mistergregorys.com; 806 N Rampart St; mains $5-13; ⏱9am-4pm;)

Mona Lisa

ITALIAN $

16 Map p30, D2

An informal and quiet local spot in the Lower Quarter, Mona Lisa is dim, dark and candlelight romantic in its own quirky way. Kooky renditions of da Vinci's familiar subject hang on the walls. Wearing hair curlers, looking 50lb heavier or appearing in the form of a cow, she stares impassively at diners munching on pizzas, pastas and spinach salads. (504-522-6746; 1212 Royal St; mains $9-18; ⏱5-10pm Mon-Thu, to 11pm Fri-Sun)

Sylvain

LOUISIANAN $$

17 Map p30, C5

This rustic yet elegant gastropub draws inspiration from the dedication to local ingredients shown by chefs such as Thomas Keller. The focus is Southern haute cuisine and excellent cocktails. Duck confit served on a bed of black-eyed peas is indicative of the gastronomic experience: rich, refined and delicious. (504-265-8123; www.sylvainnola.com; 625 Chartres St; mains $12-25; ⏱5:30-11pm Mon-Thu, to midnight Fri & Sat, to 10pm Sun, 11:30am-2:30pm Fri & Sat, 10:30am-2:30pm Sun)

Green Goddess   FUSION $$

18 ✗ Map p30, B6

Who serves lemongrass tofu over wasabi brûlée? Or South Indian pancakes and tamarind shrimp? Alongside smoked duck and (oh, man) truffle grits? Green Goddess, that's who. The Goddess combines a playful attitude to preparation with a world traveler's perspective on ingredient sourcing and a workman's ethic when it comes to actually cooking the stuff. (☏504-301-3347; www.greengoddessnola.com; 307 Exchange Pl; mains $12-20; ☺11am-9pm Wed-Sun; 🖋)

Drinking

Tonique   BAR

19 ☕ Map p30, B3

Tonique is a bartender's bar. Seriously: on a Sunday night, when the weekend rush is over, we've seen no less than three of the city's top bartenders arrive here to unwind. Why? Because this gem mixes some of the best drinks in the city, and it has a spirits menu as long as a Tolstoy novel to draw upon. (☏504-324-6045; www.bartonique.com; 820 N Rampart St; ☺noon-2am)

Molly's at the Market   PUB

20 ☕ Map p30, D3

A cop, a reporter and a tourist walk into a bar. That's not a joke, just a good description of the eclectic clientele you get at this excellent neighborhood bar. It's also the home of a fat cat that stares stonily at its booze-sodden kingdom; some kicking Irish coffee; and an urn containing the ashes of its founder. (☏504-525-5169; www.mollysat themarket.net; 1107 Decatur St; ☺10am-6am)

Latitude 29   COCKTAIL BAR

21 ☕ Map p30, C6

Jeff 'Beachbum Berry' is a tiki-bar scholar. If a drink has rum, is served in a faux-Polynesian cup or comes with an umbrella and some fruit, the man has written on it. Now, he serves said drinks from across the tropics in Latitude 29, a bar devoted to all things tiki. (☏504-609-3811; www.latitude 29nola.com; 321 N Peters St; ☺3-11pm Sun-Thu, 11am-11pm Fri & Sat)

Cane & Table

COCKTAIL BAR

22 Map p30, E3

When we heard this place served 'proto-tiki' cocktails, we'll admit our eyes inadvertently rolled. But the setting for Cane & Table – romantically faded interior and Mediterranean-style outdoor courtyard – is so stunning it's hard to knock the spot. And hey, those proto-tiki drinks are good; they mix Caribbean flavors, tropical fruits and plenty of rum. (☑504-581-1112; www.cane andtablenola.com; 1113 Decatur St; ☺5-11pm Mon-Thu, to midnight Fri & Sat)

Cosimo's

BAR

23 Map p30, C2

There aren't a ton of bars in the Quarter that we'd call neighborhood bars, but Cosimo's fits the bill. Dark wood, big windows, gambling machines, a good jukebox, pool tables and bartenders with the right amount of tender and toughness; this is simply a very fine bar, and it deserves your patronage. (☑504-522-9715; 1201 Burgundy St; ☺4pm-2am Mon & Tue, to 5am Wed-Fri, 2pm-5am Sat, 2pm-2am Sun)

Erin Rose

BAR

24 Map p30, B5

The Rose is only a block from Bourbon St, but feels a world away. Few tourists make it in here, but it's the go-to cheap spot for off-shift service folks, who hit it up for a beer, banter and a shot or five. Excellent po'boys. (☑504-522-3573; 811 Conti St; ☺24hr)

Chart Room

BAR

25 Map p30, B6

The Chart Room is simply a great bar. There's a historical patina on the walls, creaky furniture inside, outdoor seating for people-watching and a cast of characters plucked from a Mickey Spillane novel that passed through a carnival. (☑504-522-1708; 300 Chartres St; ☺11am-4am)

French 75

BAR

26 Map p30, A5

This spot is all wood and patrician accents, but the staff is friendly and down to earth. They'll mix high-quality drinks that will make you feel (a) like the star of your own Tennessee Williams play about decadent South-

---

Q Local Life

Central Grocery Muffuletta

There are a few New Orleans names inextricably linked to a certain dish, and **Central Grocery** (☑504-523-1620; 923 Decatur St; sandwiches $7-10; ☺9am-5pm Tue-Sun) is the word-association winner for the *muffuletta*. That's pronounced 'muffa-lotta,' and that sums it up: your mouth will be muffled by a hell of a lotta sandwich, stuffed with meat, cheese and olive salad. This is a real grocery by the way; fresh Italian produce is a draw on its own.

French Quarter in the evening

ern aristocracy and (b) drunk. (📞504-523-5433; www.arnaudsrestaurant.com/bars/french-75; 813 Bienville St; 🕐5:30-10pm)

Lafitte's Blacksmith Shop
BAR

27 🚇 Map p30, C3

This gutted brick cottage claims to be the oldest operating bar in the country and is certainly one of the most atmospheric in the Quarter. Rumors suggest this spot was once the workshop of pirate Jean Lafitte and his brother Pierre. Whether true or not (historical records suggest 'not'), the house dates to the 18th century.

(📞504-593-9761; www.lafittesblacksmith-shop.com; 941 Bourbon St; 🕐10:30am-3am)

Spitfire Coffee
CAFE

28 🚇 Map p30, C4

This spot specializes in pour-over coffee and espresso drinks. It serves some of the strongest java in the Quarter, eschewing the usual amounts of milk. Grab that coffee, wander over to Jackson Sq, and fuel yourself up for a caffeine-powered day of sightseeing. (www.spitfirecoffee.com; 627 St Peter St; 🕐8am-7pm Sun-Thu, to 9pm Fri & Sat)

Oz
CLUB

29 Map p30, C4

Your traditional shirtless, all-night-party, loud-music, lots-of-dancing-boys bar, where there are bowls of condoms for customers. (☎504-593-9491; www.ozneworleans.com; 800 Bourbon St; ⏱24hr)

Bourbon Pub & Parade
CLUB

30 Map p30, C4

The Bourbon is the heart of New Orleans' gay scene, or at least the nightlife and party scene. Many of the events that pepper the city's gay calendar either begin, end or are conducted here; during Southern Decadence, in particular, this is the place to be. Ladies are welcome, but this is pretty much a bar for the boys. (☎504-529-2107; www.bourbonpub.com; 801 Bourbon St; ⏱24hr)

Top Tip
Preservation Hall Prep

Preservation Hall is fantastic, but also small. One-hour sets play on the hour, and you need to show up early – an hour before – to snag a seat. Otherwise you'll be standing and, likely as not, your view will be blocked by people in front of you. When it's warm enough to leave the window shutters open, those not fortunate enough to get inside can join the crowd on the sidewalk to listen to the sets. Also note: no booze or snacks are served in the club.

Entertainment

Preservation Hall
JAZZ

31 Map p30, B4

Preservation Hall, housed in a former art gallery that dates back to 1803, is one of the most storied live-music venues in New Orleans. Barbara Reid and Grayson 'Ken' Mills formed the Society for the Preservation of New Orleans Jazz in 1961, at a time when Louis Armstrong's generation was already getting on in years. The resident performers, the Preservation Hall Jazz Band, are ludicrously talented, and regularly tour around the world. (☎504-522-2841; www.preservationhall.com; 726 St Peter St; cover Sun-Thu $15, Fri & Sat $20; ⏱showtimes 8pm, 9pm & 10pm)

Palm Court Jazz Café
LIVE MUSIC

32 Map p30, E3

Fans of trad jazz who want to hang out with a mature crowd should head to this supper-club alternative to Preservation Hall. Palm Court is a roomy venue that has a consistently good lineup of local legends; you can't go wrong if you're a jazz fan. Shows start at 8pm. (☎504-525-0200; www.palmcourt-jazzcafe.com; 1204 Decatur St; cover around $5; ⏱7-11pm Wed-Sun)

House of Blues
LIVE MUSIC

33 Map p30, B7

The House of Blues has put a lot of admirable work into making its New Orleans outpost distinctive: there's tons of folk art and rustic, voodoo-themed murals and sculptures lying about. A few doors down, HOB's small auxiliary club, the **Parish**, is a great spot; you can get pretty up-close-and-personal with artists during gigs. (📞504-310-4999; www.houseofblues.com; 225 Decatur St; tickets $7-25)

Shopping

Fifi Mahony's   BEAUTY

34 🏠 Map p30, D3

New Orleans is the most costume-crazy city in the USA, and Fifi Mahony's is the place to go to don a wig. There's a stunning selection of hairpieces here that runs the gamut from the glittered to the beehived, presented in a veritable rainbow of colors. An on-site beauty salon and sassy staff round out the experience. (📞504-525-4343; 934 Royal St; ⏱noon-6pm Sun-Fri. 11am-7pm Sat)

Green Eyed Gator   ARTS

35 🏠 Map p30, D4

Local artists and artisans have filled this gallery with odds, ends and some truly funky paintings. The prices are grounded compared to some of the fancier galleries on Royal St, and there's a general sense of playful creativity in the air. (📞504-535-4507; www.greeneyedgator.com; 901 Chartres St; ⏱11am-6pm)

Chiwawa Gaga   PET SHOP

36 🏠 Map p30, D4

It's hard not to love a pet shop specifically dedicated to costumes for small dogs. That's a bit of a niche obsession, and the folks who run this store are dedicated to sourcing, and often creating by hand, some fantastically elaborate getups for your little pooch. (📞504 581 4242; www.chiwawagaga.com; 511 Dumaine St; ⏱noon-6pm)

Esoterica Occult Goods   GIFTS

37 🏠 Map p30, D4

There are many (many) hokey magic/voodoo/spell shops in the French Quarter, but Esoterica is one of our favorites. There's a sense of sincerity regarding the occult here; folks genuinely want to help you with spells and karmic realignment. Pop in for some mystical consultation. (📞504-581-7711; www.onewitch.com; 541 Dumaine St; ⏱noon-6pm Fri-Tue, noon-3pm Wed & Thu)

Explore

Faubourg Marigny & Bywater

Live music, historical architecture, great places to eat and bars with tons of character are the foundation stones of a visit to New Orleans, and all have a strong base in Faubourg Marigny and Bywater. These neighborhoods blend bohemian sensibility with an ever-increasing quotient of hipness.

The Sights in a Day

☼ Start the day with breakfast at the **Cake Café & Bakery** (p51). You've landed yourself deep in the Marigny on Chartres St. You can lose a bit of the day just wandering around soaking up the pretty; make sure to stop by the exterior of the **Marigny Opera House** (p53), originally the 1853 Holy Trinity Catholic Church.

☼ Cross the Press St tracks and enter the Bywater. Get your afternoon started with lunch at **Pizza Delicious** (p50), or if you're willing to walk a little further, BBQ at the **Joint** (p51). Wander up Louisa St and check out the **Bywater Bargain Center** (p55) and walk along the river in the **Crescent Park** (p49).

☾ Wander back into the Marigny and stop into **Mimi's** (p52), where you may want to grab some dinner; if not here, pop into the **Lost Love** (p52), which serves great Vietnamese chow in the back. As the night wears on, wander around **Frenchmen St** (p49) and St Claude Ave; your mission is to find great live music and to soak up the bliss of a perfect New Orleans evening.

For a local's night out in the Marigny, see p46.

🔍 Local Life

A Night of Jazz & Live Music (p46)

♥ Best of New Orleans

Eating
Elizabeth's (p51)

Maurepas Foods (p51)

Bacchanal (p50)

Live Music
J.b.a. (p53)

Hi Ho Lounge (p54)

Bars & Clubs
Lost Love (p52)

Mimi's (p52)

Gay & Lesbian
Faubourg Marigny Book Store (p55)

Country Club (p52)

Getting There

🚌 **Bus** No 5 runs from Canal and Decatur Sts up Decatur and onto Poydras and Dauphine into the heart of the Marigny and Bywater.

🚗 **Car** Free street parking is plentiful in the Bywater, and only a little less common in the Marigny.

Local Life
A Night of Jazz & Live Music

OK, maybe we can't say definitively that the Marigny and the Bywater are the best neighborhoods for live music in the USA, but they sure are contenders. Here we focus on the Marigny – between the local spots on Frenchmen St, St Claude Ave and a bunch of dives, you will be more than spoiled for choice.

1 Dragon's Den
When it comes to rock, ska, punk, drum and bass, dubstep and hip-hop, the **Dragon's Den** (📞504-940-5546; www.dragonsden nola.com; 435 Esplanade Ave; ⏰8pm-2am Mon-Thu, to 5am Fri-Sun) consistently hosts some of the best acts in New Orleans. If you're hungry, hit up the on-site restaurant, **Seoul Shack**, for Korean comfort food: chicken wings, kimchi braised pork tacos and rice bowls served with hot chili slaw.

❷ Maison

Enter the Marigny proper via the live-music strip of Frenchmen St. Get your evening started at **Maison** (📞504-371-5543; www.maisonfrenchmen.com; 508 Frenchmen St; ⏰5pm-2am Sun, Tue & Wed, to 2:30am Thu, to 3am Mon & Fri, to 3:30am Sat); it's one of the fancier Frenchmen spots, and has a good mix of acts. Try one of the special house vodkas and enjoy the music, which starts on the early side.

❸ Yuki Izakaya

DJs regularly spin at **Yuki** (📞504-943-1122; 525 Frenchmen St; ⏰5pm-3am), a small bar serving up great sushi and sake. The clean taste of Japanese food and drink is a good start to a night out. Even if you're not drinking, Yuki's graphic-design interior meets vintage-film interior shouldn't be missed.

❹ Café Negril

When you spin the Frenchmen St musical wheel, **Café Negril** (📞504-944-4744; 606 Frenchmen St; ⏰7pm-1am Mon-Wed, 5pm-2am Thu-Sun) is the stop for reggae, blues, Latin and world music. If you're craving that sort of groove, and the dancing that goes with it, roll on in. If you didn't eat at Yuki, there are tasty on-site tacos served in the back.

❺ People-Watching

Frenchmen St is a consistently good spot for people-watching, even if those people do admittedly become a little rowdy on weekends. The main strip is only three blocks long, but you can view a lifetime's worth of the human tapestry on any given night: buskers, poets for hire, hustlers, the hustled, the costumed and the crazy.

❻ Phoenix Bar

It's time to head towards St Claude Ave, but don't think we're heading all the way over without a refueling go-cup drink! Head to the **Phoenix** (📞504-945-9264; www.phoenixbarnola.com; 941 Elysian Fields Ave; ⏰11am-midnight Mon-Fri, noon-2am Sat & Sun), a fantastic gay bar where the leather-and-denim community meets. Much more of a locals' scene than similar spots in the Quarter.

❼ Gene's

We know you've had a bit to eat and drink by now, so we're not necessarily saying you should stop at **Gene's** (📞504-943-3861; 1040 Elysian Fields Ave; po'boys $7; ⏰24hr), but it does mix a fine daiquiri and cook a mean hot sausage po'boy. This 24-hour pink palace has long been a lighthouse for inebriated New Orleanians seeking a port in the storm (ie a greasy sandwich).

❽ St Claude Square

At St Claude Ave and Marigny St, you'll find venues that cater to a New Orleans crowd that jukes from university student to hipster to studded punks and beyond. Acts here have a similarly broad scope. This is an area to access the music that the city's younger taste-makers are listening to.

For reviews see

⊙ Sights   p49
⊗ Eating   p50
🍷 Drinking   p52
✪ Entertainment   p53
🛍 Shopping   p54

BYWATER

Poland Ave

Lesseps St

France St

Mazant St

N Claiborne Ave

N Robertson St

N Villere St

Urquhart St

Marais St

Alvar St

Pauline St

Independence St

Congress St

Gallier St

Desire St

Piety St

N Roman St

N Derbigny St

Louisa St

Clouet St

St Vincent de Paul Cemetery

St Claude Ave

Dauphine St

Royal St

Chartres St

N Rampart St

Burgundy St

Crescent Park

Mississippi River

Feliciana St

Montegut St

Clouet St

Press St

N Ferdinand St

Franklin Ave

ST ROCH

N Claiborne Ave

N Robertson St

N Villere St

Urquhart St

Painters St

Arts St

Music St

Port St

Franklin Ave

St Roch Ave

FAUBOURG MARIGNY

Spain St

Mandeville St

Marigny St

Elysian Fields Ave

Marais St

St Claude Ave

Chartres St

Decatur St

N Peters St

Esplanade Ave

Washington Sq Park

Frenchmen St

Frenchmen Street

N Rampart St

Burgundy St

Washington Sq Park

Esplanade Ave

Decatur St

N Peters St

Ursulines

Enlargement

A Bicycle Named Desire

Elysian Fields Ave

Washington Sq Park

Frenchmen

Art Market

Royal St

Chartres St

Enlargement

0   100 m
0   0.05 miles

0   500 m
0   0.25 miles

Numbered markers:
⊗ 11
✕ 4
✕ 7
✕ 9
⊙ 1
⊗ 6 ⊙ 23
⊗ 8
25 🛍
13 🍷
✕ 5
✪ 15
⊗ 12
⊗ 14
✪ 10
⊙ 16
🛍 18
⊙ 19
⊙ 3 🛍 21
🍷 20 ⊙ 17
⊗ 24 ⊙ 2
⊙ 22

(39)
(39)
(46)

MS PHOTOS/ALAMY ©

Frenchmen Art Market (p50)

Sights

Crescent Park
PARK

1 ⊙ Map p48, D4

This waterfront park is our favorite spot in the city for taking in the Mississippi. Enter over the enormous arch at Piety and Chartres Sts and watch the fog blanket the nearby skyline. A promenade meanders past an angular metal and concrete conceptual 'wharf' (placed next to the burned remains of the former commercial wharf); one day, the path will extend to a planned performance space at Mandeville St. A dog park is located near the Mazant St entrance, which also gives disabled access. (Piety, Chartres & Mazant Sts; ⊗8am–6pm, to 7pm mid-Mar–early Nov; P 🚹 🐾)

Frenchmen Street
STREET

2 ⊙ Map p48, A2

The 'locals' Bourbon St' is how Frenchmen is usually described to those who want to know where New Orleanians listen to music. The predictable result? Frenchmen St is now packed with out-of-towners each weekend. Still, it's a ton of fun, especially on weekdays, when the crowds thin out but music still plays. Bars and clubs are arrayed back to back for several city blocks in what may well be the best concentration of live-music venues in the country. (from Esplanade Ave to Royal St)

Frenchmen Art Market
MARKET

3 Map p48, A1

Independent artists and artisans line this alleyway market, which has built a reputation as one of the finest spots in town to find a unique gift to take home as your New Orleans souvenir. 'Art,' in this case, includes clever T-shirts, hand-crafted jewelry, trinkets and, yes, a nice selection of prints and original artwork. (www.facebook.com/frenchmenartmarket; 619 Frenchmen St; ⏰7pm-1am Thu-Sun)

Eating

Bacchanal
MODERN AMERICAN $

4 Map p48, E4

From the outside, Bacchanal looks like a leaning Bywater shack; inside are racks of wine and stinky but sexy cheese. Musicians play in the garden, while cooks dispense delicious meals on paper plates from the kitchen in the back; on any given day you may try chorizo-stuffed dates or seared diver scallops that will blow your gastronomic mind. (☎504-948-9111; www.bacchanalwine.com; 600 Poland Ave; mains $8-16, cheese from $5; ⏰11am-midnight)

Red's Chinese
CHINESE $

5 Map p48, C3

Red's has upped the Chinese cuisine game in New Orleans in a big way. The chefs aren't afraid to add lashings of Louisiana flavor, yet this isn't what we'd call 'fusion' cuisine. The food is grounded deeply in spicy Szechuan flavors, which pairs well with the occasional flash of cayenne. The General Lee's chicken is stupendously good. (☎504-304-6030; www.redschinese.com; 3048 St Claude Ave; mains $8-16; ⏰noon-3pm & 5-11pm)

Pizza Delicious
ITALIAN $

6 Map p48, D4

'Pizza D's' pies are thin-crust, New York–style and *good*. The preparation is pretty simple, but the ingredients are fresh as the morning and consistently top-notch. An easy, family-friendly ambience makes for a lovely spot for casual dinner, and it serves some good beer too if you're in the mood. Vegan pizza available. The outdoor area is pet-friendly. (www.pizzadelicious.com; 617 Piety St; pizza slices

---

Understand
Plessy v Ferguson Plaque

This plaque, at the corner of Press and Royal Sts, marks the site where African American Homer Plessy, in a carefully orchestrated act of civil disobedience, tried to board a whites-only train car. That action led to the 1896 *Plessy v Ferguson* trial, which legalized segregation under the 'separate but equal' rationale. The plaque was unveiled in 2009 by Keith Plessy and Phoebe Ferguson, descendants of the opposing parties in the original trial, now friends.

from $2.25, whole pie from $15; ⊙Tue-Sun 11am-11pm; 🍴🐾👶)

Joint
BARBECUE $

7 Map p48, E4

The Joint's smoked meat has the olfactory effect of the sirens' sweet song, pulling you, the proverbial traveling sailor, off course and into savory meat-induced blissful death (classical Greek analogies ending *now*). Knock back some ribs, pulled pork or brisket with some sweet tea in the backyard garden and learn to love life. (📞504-949-3232; www.alwaysSmokin.com; 701 Mazant St; mains $7-17; ⊙11.30am-10pm Mon-Sat)

Maurepas Foods
AMERICAN $

8 Map p48, D3

Maurepas isn't your typical Bywater spot. It's got high ceilings, minimalist decor, polished floors and metal fixtures. And boy is the food good! Try the organic chicken, market greens, grits and poached egg – all delicious. Vegetarians should snack on the soba noodles, and everyone should get drunk on the craft cocktails. (📞504-267-0072; www.maurepasfoods.com; 3200 Burgundy St; mains $7-18; ⊙5pm-midnight Mon-Fri, 10am-midnight Sat & Sun; 🍴)

Elizabeth's
CAJUN, CREOLE $$

9 Map p48, D4

Elizabeth's is deceptively divey, but the food's as good as the best New Orleans chefs can offer. This is a quintessential New Orleans experience: all friendli-

 Top Tip

Life in the Bike Lane

These neighborhoods contain a large concentration of cyclists, but roads run the gamut from smooth to pot-holed and pockmarked. The St Claude Ave cycle lane is smooth, but this is a major traffic thoroughfare. Riding here, especially at night, can feel harrowing, and there have been a number of fatal accidents.

We stress that hundreds of people use this lane safely on a daily basis, but if the traffic makes you nervous, consider riding along Chartres St – between Press St and Poland Ave; Chartres is quite smooth and relatively un-trafficked.

ness, smiling sass, weird artistic edges and overindulgence on the food front. Brunch and breakfast are top draws – the praline bacon is no doubt sinful but consider us happily banished from the Garden. (📞504-944-9272; www.elizabethsrestaurantnola.com; 601 Gallier St; mains $16-26; ⊙8am-2.30pm & 6-10pm Mon-Sat, 8am-2.30pm Sun)

Cake Café & Bakery
BREAKFAST $

10 Map p48, B3

On weekend mornings the line is quite literally out the door here. Biscuits and gravy (topped with andouille), fried oysters and grits (seasonally available) and all the omelets are standouts. Lunch is great, too, as are the cakes (king cake!) whipped up in the back. (📞504-943-0010; www.nolacakes.com; 2440 Chartres St; mains $6-11; ⏱7am-3pm Wed-Mon)

Drinking

BJ's
BAR

11 🍷 Map p48, E3

This Bywater dive attracts a neighborhood crowd seeking cheap beers, chilled-out banter and occasional live music, especially the Monday blues-rock show by King James & the Special Men, which starts around 10pm. How great is this place? Robert Plant felt the need to put on an impromptu set here the last time he visited town. (📞504-945-9256; 4301 Burgundy St; ⏱5pm-late)

Mimi's in the Marigny
BAR

12 🍷 Map p48, B3

The name of this bar could justifiably change to 'Mimi's *is* the Marigny';

we can't imagine the neighborhood without this institution. Mimi's is as attractively disheveled as Brad Pitt on a good day, all comfy furniture, pool tables, an upstairs dance hall decorated like a Creole mansion gone punk, and dim, brown lighting like a fantasy in sepia. (📞504-872-9868; 2601 Royal St; ⏱6pm-2am Sun-Thu, to 4am Fri & Sat)

Country Club
BAR

13 🍷 Map p48, C4

From the front, it's a well-decorated Bywater house. Walk inside and there's a restaurant, sauna, leafy patio with bar, heated outdoor pool, 25ft projector screen and a hot tub! There's a $10 towel rental fee if you want to hang in the pool area, which is a popular carousing spot for the gay and lesbian community (all sexualities welcome). (📞504-945-0742; www.thecountryclubneworleans.com; 634 Louisa St; ⏱bar 10am-1am, restaurant 11am-9pm Sun-Thu, to 10pm Fri & Sat)

Lost Love
BAR

14 🍷 Map p48, B3

Dark and sexy, the Lost Love is that vampy Marigny girl or moody artist your momma told you to stay away from, mixed with a bit of blue-collar dive-bar sensibility. Don't listen to her. The drinks are cheap and the pours are strong plus there's regular karaoke and HBO shows on a projector, and an excellent Vietnamese kitchen in the back. (📞504-949-2009; www.lostlovelounge.com; 2529 Dauphine St; ⏱6pm-midnight)

Local Life
Clouet Gardens

This formerly empty lot has been transformed by its Bywater neighbors into a wonderful little **park** (www.clouetgardens.org; 707 Clouet St; ⏱sunrise-sunset; 👫👶) filled with public art projects, murals and generally appealing weirdness. Performances, concerts and neighborhood get-togethers are frequently held here, and it's a favorite with local families.

CHRIS BULL/ALAMY ©

Spotted Cat (p54)

Entertainment

Marigny Opera House

PERFORMING ARTS

15 Map p48, C3

This former church has been remodeled into a performing-arts space that's infused with the sort of romantic dilapidation that very much fits the New Orleans aesthetic. The Opera House gained national prominence when Solange Knowles (Beyonce's sister) got married here; on other days, the venue hosts theater and music and showcases its own dance company. (☎504-948-9998; www.marignyoperahouse. org; 725 St Ferdinand St)

AllWays Lounge

THEATER

16 Map p48, A2

In a city full of funky music venues, the AllWays stands out as one of the funkiest. On any given night of the week you may see experimental guitar, local theater, thrashy rock, live comedy or a '60s-inspired shagadelic dance party. Also: the drinks are supercheap. (☎504-218-5778; www. theallwayslounge.net; 2240 St Claude Ave; ☉6pm-midnight Sat-Wed, to 2am Thu & Fri)

d.b.a.

LIVE MUSIC

17 Map p48, A1

Swank d.b.a. consistently schedules some of the best live music in town. Listening to John Boutté's sweet tenor, which sounds like birds making love on the Mississippi, is one of the best beginnings to a night in New Orleans. Brass bands, rock shows, blues – everything plays here. Plus, there's an amazing beer selection. Seriously d.b.a., you freaking *win*. (☎504-942-3731; www.dbaneworleans.com; 618 Frenchmen St; ⊙5pm-4am Mon-Thu, from 4pm Fri-Sun; 🛜)

Hi Ho Lounge
LIVE MUSIC

18 ⭐ Map p48, A2

Alt-country, folk, rock, punk, brass bands, dance parties and Mardi Gras Indians regularly pop up at the Hi Ho. It can get pretty packed, but this remains one of the best mid-sized venues in town for a live act. (☎504-945-4446; www.hiholounge.net; 2239 St Claude Ave; ⊙6pm-2am Sun-Thu, to 3am Fri & Sat)

Spotted Cat
LIVE MUSIC

19 ⭐ Map p48, A1

It's good the Spotted Cat is across the street from Snug Harbor. They're both great jazz clubs, but where the latter is a swish martini sorta spot, the former is a thumping sweatbox where drinks are served in plastic cups – an ideal execution of the tiny New Orleans music club. (www.spottedcatmusicclub.com; 623 Frenchmen St; ⊙4pm-2am Mon-Fri, from 3pm Sat & Sun)

Snug Harbor
JAZZ

20 ⭐ Map p48, A1

There may be bigger venues but, overall, Snug Harbor is the best jazz club in the city. That's partly because it usually hosts doubleheaders, giving you a good dose of variety, and partly because the talent is kept to an admirable mix of reliable legends and hot up-and-comers; in the course of one night you'll likely witness both. (☎504-949-0696; www.snugjazz.com; 626 Frenchmen St; ⊙5-11pm)

Shopping

I.J. Reilly's
HANDICRAFTS

21 🔒 Map p48, B1

How deeply New Orleans is this store? It's named for Ignatious Reilly, protagonist of *A Confederacy of Dunces,* and located in the Kowalski house from *A Streetcar Named Desire.* Inside, the shop sells all manner of clever New

Orleans gifts, from photography books to printed screens and local artwork. (☎504-304-7928; www.ijreillys.squarespace.com; 632 Elysian Fields Ave; ⊘10am-5pm Wed-Mon)

Louisiana Music Factory   MUSIC

22 Map p48, A4

Where else would you find one of the best repositories of New Orleans and Louisiana music than the head of Frenchmen St? The Louisiana Music Factory, besides boasting racks of local music (and a staff that loves to chat about said music), also frequently hosts concerts on its sales floor. (☎504-586-1094; www.louisianamusicfactory.com; 421 Frenchmen St; ⊘11am-8pm Sun-Thu, to 10pm Fri & Sat)

Euclid Records   MUSIC

23 Map p48, D4

New Orleans is the kind of town that deserves really cool record shops, and Euclid is happy to oblige. It's got all the ingredients: racks of rare vinyl, old concert posters, a knowledge-able staff that looks plucked from a Nick Hornby novel (except they're all friendly, eschewing the music-snob stereotype) and a board listing what-ever live music you should see while

in town. (☎504-947-4348; www.euclid-nola.com; 3301 Chartres St; ⊘11am-7pm)

Faubourg Marigny Book Store   BOOKS

24 Map p48, A2

The South's oldest gay bookstore is a ramshackle, intellectual spot, and a good place to pick up local 'zines and catch up on the New Orleans scene, gay or otherwise. Look for the subtle (enormous) rainbow flag. (☎504-947-3700; www.fabontrenchmen.com; 600 Frenchmen St; ⊘noon-10pm)

Bywater Bargain Center   ANTIQUES

25 Map p48, C3

This emporium is a treasure trove of, well, treasures, if you follow the old adage that one person's junk is another's...well, you know. There are found objects, old door frames, handmade crafts, plaster alligators playing zydeco and who knows what else. Most impressive is a collection of Mexican folk art, including Oaxacan sculpture and Día de los Muertos (Day of the Dead) paraphernalia. (☎504-948-0007; 3200 Dauphine St; ⊘11am-6pm)

Explore

CBD & Warehouse District

The Central Business District (CBD) and Warehouse District are, architecturally, the least typical neighborhoods in New Orleans. You will find older row houses, town houses and (of course) warehouses, but you'll also find skyscrapers and the like. No matter – in between lie concert halls, art galleries, restaurants, grand hotels and the finest collection of museums in the city.

The Sights in a Day

☀ In the morning, go have breakfast at **Ruby Slipper** (p69) before exploring the **National WWII Museum** (p58). Your visit here can easily eat up the whole day, so try and hit your must-see list of exhibits. When you're done, have a walk around the Warehouse District and stop by the **Preservation Resource Center** (p66) for a quick immersion into New Orleans architecture.

☀ Grab lunch at **Cochon** (p67) or, if you're feeling more casual, **Cochon Butcher** (p68). Then you have a decision to make: do you want the studies in regional artwork and outsider art that make up the **Ogden Museum of Southern Art** (p60), or the fascinating curated exhibits at the **Contemporary Arts Center** (p66)? Don't forget oyster happy hour at **Luke** (p68), which happens daily from 3pm to 6pm!

☾ Try and book a dinner at **Peche Seafood Grill** (p66) or **Restaurant August** (p67); the former is, quite simply, one of the best seafood restaurants in the nation, while the latter does masterful takes on haute New Orleans cuisine. After you've gorged on some fine dining, take in a show at the **Howlin' Wolf** (p71) or the **Circle Bar** (p69).

For a local's day gallery-hopping in the Arts District, see p62.

👁 Top Sights

National WWII Museum (p58)

Ogden Museum of Southern Art (p60)

🔍 Local Life

Gallery-Hopping in the Arts District (p62)

♥ Best of New Orleans

Eating

Carmo (p69)

Restaurant August (p67)

Museums

National WWII Museum (p58)

Ogden Museum of Southern Art (p60)

Architecture

National WWII Museum (p58)

Getting There

🚗 **Car** From the airport, exit off the elevated US 90; from the east, exit off the I-10.

🚕 **Taxi & shuttle** A cab from the airport costs $33 for one or two people; shuttles $20 per person.

🚆 **Train & bus** The Amtrak and Greyhound stations border Loyola Ave. The Loyola-UPT streetcar line runs from the stations to Canal St.

◉ Top Sights
National WWII Museum

The National WWII Museum is both a wide-lens retrospective and a deeply intimate reckoning of the largest conflict in history. Wall-sized photographs suggest the confusion of D-Day; oral histories tell remarkable stories of survival; and a stroll through the snowy woods of Ardennes feels eerily cold. Exhibits like these make this facility, which opened in 2000 as the National D-Day Museum, so engaging: the grand sweep of history is humanized and accessed through personal recollections and heat-of-the-action displays.

◉ Map p64, E5

☏ 504-528-1944

www.nationalww2museum.org

945 Magazine St

adult/child/senior $23/14/20, plus 1/2 films $5/10

⊘ 9am-5pm

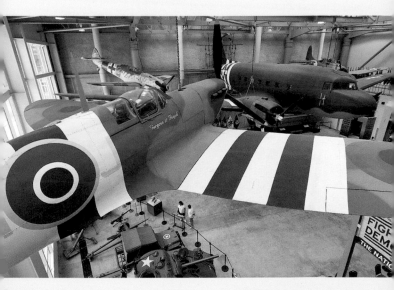

Don't Miss

Regular Exhibits

Visitors can personalize their exploration by registering for a dog tag, which connects them with the same WWII participant at various exhibits. The central Campaigns of Courage pavilion spotlights the European and Pacific theaters; the *Road to Berlin* and *Road to Tokyo* exhibitions (the latter opening December 2015) are immersive journeys along the course of the war from the American perspective.

4D Movie

Beyond All Boundaries takes a 4D look at America's involvement in the war on a 120ft-wide screen. Get ready for rumbling seats and a dusting of snowflakes! The movie shows daily from 10am to 4pm, Sunday to Thursday, with an additional 5pm showing on Friday and Saturday. It's a 45-minute movie with a seven-minute pre-show; plan accordingly.

USS Tang

Final Mission: The USS Tang Experience takes visitors into an interior replica of submarine USS *Tang* and puts them through the paces of its harrowing fifth and final voyage. This is a separate ticketed event running daily from 9:35am to 4:35pm Sunday to Thursday (to 5:35pm Friday and Saturday); buy tickets on the museum website.

Stage Door Canteen

The whole theme of 1940s immersion gets the entertainment treatment at the Stage Door, which features regular performances adapting the era's croony boogie-woogie vintage sound. Buy show tickets in advance via the museum's website. The name derives from a World War II–era club for Allied servicemen, and a movie made about it.

☑ **Top Tips**

▶ The museum is pretty big. Give yourself at least 2½ hours to do it justice.

▶ Buy tickets in advance for shows at the Stage Door Canteen.

▶ Behind-the-scenes tours ($345/650 per person/couple) on Fridays give you access to artifacts not displayed in the museum.

✕ **Take a Break**

If you need a break and a bite to eat, head to the Americana-themed, and appropriately named, on-site **American Sector** (www.nationalww2museum.org/american-sector; mains lunch $10-14, dinner $14-28; ⊙11am-9pm) restaurant.

Need a drink and some live music? We're always fans of the Circle Bar (p69), located off nearby Lee Circle.

Top Sights
Ogden Museum of Southern Art

The Ogden Museum sits just a few steps away from the city's iconic statue of Robert E Lee, but this vibrant collection of Southern art isn't stuck in the past. The museum manages to be beautiful, educational and unpretentious all at once. The galleries, split over five floors, hold pieces that range from impressionist landscapes and outsider folk art to contemporary installation work. The Ogden is affiliated with the Smithsonian Institute in Washington, DC, giving it access to that bottomless collection.

👁 Map p64, E5

📞504-539-9650

www.ogdenmuseum.org

925 Camp St

adult/child 5-17yr/student $10/5/8

🕙10am-5pm Wed-Mon, plus 5:30-8pm Thu

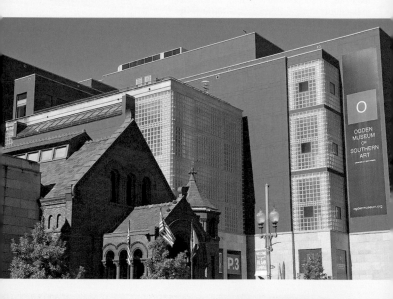

Don't Miss

Entrance Atrium

The glass-and-stone Stephen Goldring Hall, with its soaring atrium, provides an inspiring welcome to the grounds and forms the focal point of the museum. The building is home to the museum's 20th- and 21st-century exhibitions as well as the Museum Store. 'Floating' stairs between floors lead visitors through the permanent and changing collections.

Permanent Collection

Some of our favorite elements of the permanent collection include a stunning collection of self-taught 'outsider' art on the top floor of the museum; a collection of Southern landscapes that explores the region's fascination with its geography; and an excellent grouping of 20th-century Southern regionalists.

Ogden After Hours

On Thursday nights, pop in for Ogden After Hours. You can access the museum's exhibitions (barring special collections) while enjoying thoughtfully curated live performances in the main lobby. The acts aren't stereotypically what you'd expect in a museum; this is New Orleans, after all, and you may catch some truly danceable music. Shows cost $6.25, and go from 6pm to 8pm.

Museum Store

If you're the type to immediately skip a museum gift store, we recommend giving the Ogden's attached shop a chance. It showcases books on, and stocks plenty of examples of, Southern arts, crafts and graphic design. If you're looking for a meaningful souvenir or gift from New Orleans that is *of* New Orleans, this is a great option.

☑ Top Tips

▶ Head to the top floor first, then make your way down to the lobby.

▶ Come for the after-hours show. You get the experience of the museum coupled with a concert. And wine!

▶ Changing exhibitions make up much of the Ogden's content; check online to see what's on display during your visit.

✗ Take a Break

For a delicious dip into modern Louisiana cuisine head to Herbsaint (p68), a two-block walk from the museum.

The sandwiches at Cochon Butcher (p68) are the stuff of legend, and they're just a five-minute walk away.

Local Life
Gallery-Hopping in the Arts District

New Orleans' ever-burgeoning Arts District (www.neworleansarts district.com) holds the most impressive concentration of serious galleries in the city. Many of them are located on Julia St. Drop by any of them to pick up a free map and guide to the district's art dealers. The neighborhood Art Walk is held the first Saturday of the month between 6pm and 9pm.

① Jean Bragg Gallery

The 'Food Court' collection, with its small paintings of beignets, shrimp and other Louisiana fare, will make your stomach growl at the jam-packed **Jean Bragg Gallery of Southern Art** (☎504-895-7375; www.jeanbragg.com; 600 Julia St; ⏱10am-5pm Mon-Sat). This welcoming gallery is a good source for the arts-and-crafts-style Newcomb Pottery. Bragg also deals in classic landscapes by Louisiana painters.

❷ REpurposing NOLA

Local entrepreneur Traci L Claussen at **REpurposingNOLA Piece by Peace** (www.repurposingnola.com; 604 Julia St; ☺11am-5pm Mon & Thu-Sat) makes you feel better, both through her products and her mission. She designs eye-catching but functional totes and similar goods from excess material, such as burlap coffee sacks and other found materials, all sewn by local seamstresses.

❸ Alex Beard Studio

Check out the intriguing drawings and lively paintings of traveler **Alex Beard** (www.alexbeardstudio.com; 608 Julia St) at his studio. From puzzles to illustrations to fine art, his adventures in 'abstract realism' will pull you in for a closer look. Much of his work has a fantastical element that wouldn't feel out of place in a cool children's storybook.

❹ George Schmidt Gallery

New Orleans artist George Schmidt, a member of the New Leviathan Oriental Fox-Trot Orchestra and the owner of the **George Schmidt Gallery** (☎504-592 0206; www.georgeschmidt.com; 626 Julia St; ☺12:30-4:30pm Tue-Sat), describes himself as a 'historical' painter. Indeed, his canvases evoke the city's past, awash in a warm, romantic light. His Mardi Gras paintings are worth a look.

❺ Ariodante

Looking for a creative gift crafted with a lot of local flavor? It's hard to leave **Ariodante** (www.ariodantegallery.com; 535 Julia St; ☺10am-5pm Mon-Sat) empty-handed. This small but well-stocked 'contemporary craft' gallery sells jewelry, glass works, ceramics and fine art by local and regional artists. The shop has held down this corner of Julia St for more than two decades.

❻ Arthur Roger Gallery

One of the district's most prominent galleries, **Arthur Roger** (☎504-522-1999; www.arthurrogergallery.com; 432 Julia St; ☺10am-5pm Mon-Sat) represents several dozen artists, including Simon Gunning, whose landscapes are haunting records of Louisiana's disappearing wetlands. The gallery is known for cultivating some of the finest talent in the region, and frequently updates its lineup of excellent artists.

❼ Soren Christensen Gallery

The impressive **Soren Christensen Gallery** (☎504-569-9501; www.sorengallery.com; 400 Julia St; ☺10am-5:30pm Tue-Fri, 11am-5pm Sat) showcases the work of nationally renowned painters, photographers and sculptors; that last genre is worth noting, as area galleries tend to be light on sculpture.

❽ Lemieux Galleries

Gulf Coast art is the emphasis in the nationally recognized **Lemieux Galleries** (☎504-522-5988; www.lemieuxgalleries.com; 332 Julia St; ☺10am-6pm Mon-Sat). It's a good place to get a handle on the breadth of the regional arts scene. Works here include Shirley Rabe Masinter's realistic paintings of New Orleans – note the wonderful local signage – and Jon Langford's depictions of local musicians.

For reviews see

⦿ Top Sights	p58
⦿ Sights	p66
⊗ Eating	p66
🍷 Drinking	p69
✪ Entertainment	p71
🔒 Shopping	p71

E

Iberville St
Bienville St
Bourbon St
Royal St
Exchange Pl

F

Chartres St

G

FRENCH QUARTER

Decatur St
Clinton St
N Peters St
Clay St
N Front St

Bienville

Moonwalk

H

1

9
Baronne St
Bourbon St/
Carondelet St

Canal St

Chartres St/
Camp St

Woldenberg Park

Common St
19

Gravier St
Common St

Shops at
Canal Place

Peters St

2

Union St   Union St
6
Perdido St

Camp St
Magazine St
Tchoupitoulas St
S Peters St

Canal St
Wharf

Canal

Ferry to Algiers

Mississippi River

Poydras
4

Natchez St

Harrah's
Casino

World
Trade
Centre

Spanish
Plaza

3

N Maestri

Poydras St

Poydras St

Poydras

Lafayette
Sq
S Maestri

US
Courthouse

Constance St

Piazza
D'Italia

Lafayette St

Convention Center Blvd

8
St Charles Ave
Church St
Camp St

Capdeville St
14

Girod St

Riverwalk
Mall

4

Julia
Julia Row

16

Julia St
Magazine St

10
Julia St

Notre Dame St

Ogden Museum
of Southern Art

3

Constance St
Tchoupitoulas St
Commerce St

**WAREHOUSE
DISTRICT**

18

Fulton St

13
1 Contemporary
Arts Center

**National WWII
Museum**

Andrew Higgins Dr

15 Preservation
Resource
Center

St Joseph St

5 N Diamond St
7

17

Ernest N Morial
Convention
Center

5

Sights

Contemporary
Arts Center
ARTS CENTER

1 Map p64, E5

From the outside, the CAC is pretty un-assuming. But once inside, the grand modernist entrance, an airy, spacious vault with soaring ceilings and con-ceptual metal and wooden accents, is impressive. The best reason to visit? A good crop of rotating exhibitions by local as well as international artists, plus a packed events calendar that in-cludes plays, skits, dance and concerts. (CAC; ✆504-528-3805; www.cacno.org; 900 Camp St; adult/student/child $10/8/free; ⏰11am-5pm Wed-Mon)

Preservation
Resource Center
HISTORIC BUILDING

2 Map p64, F5

If you're interested in the architecture of New Orleans or a self-guided walking tour, then start here. The welcoming Preservation Resource Center, located inside the 1853 Leeds-Davis building, offers free pamphlets with walking-tour maps for virtually every part of town. Helpful staff shares information about everything from cycling routes to renovating a historic home. Check the website for details about the Shotgun House tour in March and the popular Holiday Home tour in December. (✆504-581-7032; www.prcno.org; 923 Tchoupi-toulas St; admission free; ⏰9am-5pm Mon-Fri)

Eating

Peche Seafood Grill
SEAFOOD $

3 Map p64, F4

We're not sure why, but there is a split opinion locally about this latest ven-ture from Donald Link. Put us firmly in the lick-the-plate and order-more category. Coastal seafood dishes are prepared simply here, but unexpected flourishes – whether from salt, spices

---

Understand
Andrew Higgins

So why is the National WWII Museum located in New Orleans, and not Wash-ington, DC? And why is it on Andrew Higgins Dr? The answers are connected, because from 2000 to 2003 the museum was named the National D-Day Museum, and Andrew Higgins was a crucial figure in the Normandy landings.

Higgins was a New Orleans–based industrialist and inventor of the Higgins Boat. Originally designed to transport goods across marshy Louisiana, the boat was converted into the famed LCVP: the 'Landing Craft, Vehicle, Person-nel' that brought Allied soldiers to shore from the Pacific theater to Sicily and Normandy.

PANORAMIC IMAGES/GETTY IMAGES ©

Aquarium of the Americas (p68)

or magic – sear the deliciousness onto your taste buds. The vibe is convivial, with a happy, stylish crowd sipping and savoring among the exposed-brick walls and wooden beams (☎504-522 1744; www.pecherestaurant.com; 800 Magazine St; small plates $9-14, mains $14 27; ⏰11am-10pm Mon-Thu, to 11pm Fri & Sat)

Restaurant August CREOLE $$$

4 Map p64, F3

For a little romance, reserve a table at Restaurant August, the flagship of chef John Besh's nine-restaurant empire. This converted 19th-century tobacco warehouse, with its flickering candles and warm, soft shades, earns a nod for most aristocratic dining room in New

Orleans, but somehow manages to be both intimate and lively. Delicious meals take you to another level of gastronomic perception. (☎504-299-9777; www.restaurantaugust.com; 301 Tchoupitoulas St; lunch $23-36, dinner $33-42; ⏰5-10pm daily, 11am 2pm Fri & Sun; 🖘)

Cochon CAJUN $$

5 Map p64, F5

The phrase 'everything but the squeal' springs to mind when perusing the menu at Cochon, regularly named one of New Orleans' best restaurants. At this bustling eatery Donald Link pays homage to his Cajun culinary roots, and the menu revels in most parts of the pig, including pork cheeks with

Local Life
Aquarium of the Americas

Part of the Audubon Institute, the immense **Aquarium of the Americas** (☎504-581-4629; www.audubon-institute.org; 1 Canal St; adult/child $24/18; ☺10am-5pm Tue-Sun; ⛴) is loosely regional, with exhibits that delve beneath the surface of the Mississippi River, Gulf of Mexico, Caribbean Sea and far-off Amazon rainforest. The impressive Great Maya Reef lures visitors into a 30ft-long clear tunnel running through a 'submerged' Mayan city, home to rainbow clouds of exotic fish.

creole cream cheese and fried boudin. Other meats include rabbit, alligator and oysters. (☎504-588-2123; www.cochonrestaurant.com; 930 Tchoupitoulas St; small plates $8-14, mains $19-26; ☺11am-10pm Mon-Thu, to 11pm Fri & Sat)

Luke   BISTRO $$$

6 🍴 Map p64, E2

John Besh's letter of love to the working-class bistro has an elegantly simple tiled interior and a menu that will make you reconsider the limits of Louisiana-French fusion; the primary muse is the smoky, rich cuisine of Alsace, the France/Germany border. Vanilla-scented duck with lavender honey, white-bean cassoulet and an admirable nod to German meats such as *Bockwurst* all give us the pleasurable shivers. (☎504-378-2840; www.lukeneworleans.com; 333 St Charles Ave; mains $16-31; ☺7am-11pm)

Cochon Butcher   SANDWICHES $

7 🍴 Map p64, F5

Tucked behind the slightly more formal Cochon, this newly expanded sandwich and meat shop calls itself a 'swine bar & deli.' We call it our favorite sandwich shop in the city, if not the entire South. From the convivial lunch crowds to the savory sandwiches to the fun-loving cocktails, this welcoming place from local restaurant maestro Donald Link encapsulates the best of New Orleans. (www.cochonbutcher.com; 930 Tchoupitoulas St; mains $10-12; ☺10am-10pm Mon-Thu, to 11pm Fri & Sat, to 4pm Sun)

Herbsaint   MODERN LOUISIANAN $$

8 🍴 Map p64, E4

Herbsaint's duck and andouille gumbo might be the best restaurant gumbo in town. The rest of the food ain't too bad either – it's very much modern bistro fare with dibs and dabs of Louisiana influence, courtesy of owner Donald Link. Currently, the fried catfish comes with green rice and chilies, while the shrimp and grits are joined with tasso-stewed collard greens. (☎504-524-4114; www.herbsaint.com; 701 St Charles Ave; mains lunch $14-20, dinner $27-30; ☺11:30am-10pm Mon-Fri, from 5:30pm Sat)

Domenica   ITALIAN $$

9 🍴 Map p64, E1

With its wooden refectory tables, white lights and soaring ceiling, Domenica feels like a village trattoria gone posh. The 'rustic' pizza pies at this lively, often-recommended spot are loaded with nontraditional but enticing toppings – clams, prosciutto, smoked pork – and are big enough that solo diners should have a slice or two left over. (☑504-648-6020; 123 Baronne St; mains $13-30; ☺11am-11pm; ☑)

Carmo
HEALTH FOOD, SANDWICHES **$**

10 Map p64, E4

Need a break from boudin balls, red beans and rice, and heavy cream sauces? Step into this no-fuss cafe for creative salads, sandwiches, raw fish creations, and vegetarian and vegan dishes – most with a tropical spin. The popular Rico comes as a salad or sandwich with pulled pork or vegan 'meat' plus cheese, avocado, salsa and a kicky sauce. Numerous fruit juices are available, too. Order at the counter. (☑504-875-4132; www.cafecarmo.com; 527 Julia St; mains lunch $9-12, dinner $9-15; ☺11am-3pm Mon, to 10pm Tue & Wed, to 11pm Thu-Sat; ☑)

Ruby Slipper – Downtown
BREAKFAST **$**

11 Map p64, F2

This rapidly growing local chain specializes in down-home Southern breakfasts prepared with decadent oomph. How does fried chicken on a biscuit with poached eggs and tasso cream sauce sound? Soon after the doors open in the morning this lively joint is full up with solos, families, college-age kids, renegade convention-goers and folks revving up before the party that is New Orleans. (www.

therubyslippercafe.net; 200 Magazine St; mains $8-14; ☺7am-2pm Mon-Fri, 8am-2pm Sat, 8am-3pm Sun)

Drinking

Circle Bar
BAR

12 Map p64, D5

Picture a grand Victorian mansion, all disheveled and punk, and you've caught the essence of this strangely inviting place to drink. Live acts of varying quality – folk, rock and indie – occupy the central space, where a little fireplace and lots of grime speak to the coziness of one of New Orleans' great dives. The house teeters on Lee Circle, across from a somber statue of General Lee. (☑504-588-2616; 1032 St Charles Ave; ☺4pm-late, shows 10pm)

Local Life
Mardi Gras World

We dare say that **Mardi Gras World** (☑504-361-7821; www.mardigrasworld. com; 1380 Port of New Orleans Pl; adult/child 2-11yr $20/13; ☺tours 9:30am-4:30pm; ☑) is one of the happiest places in New Orleans by day – but at night it must turn into one of the most terrifying funhouses this side of Hell. It's all those faces, man, the dragons, clowns, kings and fairies, all leering and dead-eyed... Maybe it's just us. That said, we love touring the studio warehouse of Blaine Kern (Mr Mardi Gras) and family, who have been making parade floats since 1947. Tours last 30 to 45 minutes.

Bellocq
COCKTAIL BAR

13 Map p64, E5

White candles, plush Victorian chairs, intimate nooks, deep purples and blacks – Bellocq has a boudoir style well-suited to upscale vampires in the mood for brooding. Named for a pre-prohibition maritime photographer who secretly snapped photos of local madams, Bellocq pays homage to the golden age of drink with 'cobblers' and other 1800s-inspired cocktails. (www.thehotelmodern.com/bellocq; 936 St Charles Ave; ☺5pm-midnight Mon-Thu, 4pm-2am Fri & Sat, to 10pm Sun)

Capdeville
BAR

14 🚇 Map p64, F4

The compact Capdeville is an upscale pub with retro roots – check out that

jukebox and the album covers – on the 1st floor of the Intellectual Property building just off Lafayette Sq. After a stroll past the Julia St galleries or a date in the Federal District Court, pop in for a whiskey or Guinness at the elevated bar. (www.capdevillenola.com; 520 Capdeville St; ☺11am-2:30pm & 5-11pm Mon-Thu, 11am-midnight Fri & Sat)

Rusty Nail
BAR

15 🚇 Map p64, F5

The Rusty Nail is a dive bar for newbies. Yeah, it lurks in a dark spot under the I-90 overpass, but it's also flanked by loft complexes that look downright trendy. The twinkling white lights are kinda cute, too. And, heck, on Thursdays it hosts a trivia night. Come on in, have a beer or a scotch (there's a long list), and kick back. (☎504-525-5515; www.therustynail.biz; 1100 Constance St; ☺4pm-1am Mon-Thu, 2pm-3am Fri, noon-3am Sat, noon-1am Sun)

Lucy's Retired Surfers Bar
BAR

16 🚇 Map p64, F4

There's always somebody sipping a drink at one of the sidewalk tables at Lucy's, a beach-bum kinda spot oddly plopped in the middle of downtown. It draws the twenty- and thirty-something crowd but it's also decent for an after-work drink. Have something colorful and cold, and we'll see you at the next bar. Closing time varies. (☎504-523-8995; www.lucys

Top Tip

Street Parking in the CBD

Free parking is nearly impossible to find downtown, and parking meters typically run from 8am to 6pm Monday through Saturday. Sidewalk parking kiosks that accept coins and credit/debit cards are common, but you'll still find plenty of the old coin-gobbling meters. If you're out of coins but parked at a coin-meter spot, you can still use your debit or credit card to get a receipt from one of the kiosks. Place the receipt on your dashboard. Double-check all signs for variances.

retiredsurfers.com; 701 Tchoupitoulas St;
⊘11am-late Mon-Fri, 10am-late Sat & Sun)

Entertainment

Howlin' Wolf

LIVE MUSIC

17 ⭐ Map p64, G5

One of New Orleans' best venues for
live blues, alt-rock, jazz and roots
music, the Howlin' Wolf draws a lively
crowd. It started out booking local
progressive bands, but has become
a stop for bigger-name touring acts
such as Hank Williams III and Alison
Krauss. The club is now offering comedy acts on Tuesdays and Thursdays.
(☎504-522-9653; www.thehowlinwolf.com;
907 S Peters St; cover free-$35; ⊘hours
vary)

Republic New Orleans

LIVE MUSIC

18 ⭐ Map p64, G5

Republic showcases some pretty
awesome live acts, including George
Clinton and other good funk and
blues talent, but it's also a place
where teenagers from the burbs
come to behave very badly. There's
your conundrum: your night may
consist of a potentially great show,
but there's a good chance it will also
include screeching, jostling teens.
Most shows start at 10pm. (☎504-
528-8282; www.republicnola.com; 828 S
Peters St; cover $10-50; ⊘hours vary)

Saxophonist, New Orleans

Shopping

Meyer the Hatter

ACCESSORIES

19 🔒 Map p64, E2

This cluttered shop a half-block from
Canal St has a truly astounding inven-
tory of world-class hats. Biltmore,
Dobbs and Stetson are just a few of
the milliners represented. Fur felts
dominate in fall and winter, and
flimsy straw hats take over in spring
and summer. The selection of lids for
the ladies seemed a wee bit skimpy
on our last visit. (☎504-525-1048; www.
meyerthehatter.com; 120 St Charles Ave;
⊘10am-5:45pm Mon-Sat)

Explore

Garden & Lower Garden Districts

In the Garden and Lower Garden Districts you'll find both elegant mansions and long boulevards that are packed with some of the city's finest dining and shopping, particularly around Magazine St. The enormous boughs of ancient live oak trees provide shade. The area's demographic is a mix of students and the city's aristocratic elite.

The Sights in a Day

☀ Start the day right with break-fast at **Surrey's** (p81), one of our favorite places to begin any day, ever. Then head to Central City and walk along Oretha Castle-Haley Blvd, soaking up one of the fastest-growing urban renewal corridors in the city. As you make your way back to the Lower Garden District, consider stopping at the **McKenna Museum of African American Art** (p80).

☀ Walk back to Magazine St and grab a tasty deli sandwich for lunch at **Stein's** (p82). Wander around, popping into the **Irish Channel** (p80), where a Guinness at **Parasol's** (p82) is the done thing. This part of town is really pretty, especially along St Charles Ave. After walking that green stretch, take Washington Ave back towards Magazine St and explore **Lafayette Cemetery No 1** (p74).

☾ Have dinner at **Coquette** (p82) and finish the day along Maga-zine St. The best shopping strip in the city comes alive during the evening, as a young crowd starts to wend between numerous bars, cafes and restaurants. Enjoy an outdoor courtyard beer at the **Bulldog** (p84).

For a local's day shopping on Magazine St, see p76.

◉ **Top Sights**

Lafayette Cemetery No 1 (p74)

Q **Local Life**

Shopping on Magazine Street (p76)

♥ **Best of New Orleans**

Eating

Surrey's Juice Bar (p81)

Stein's Deli (p82)

Bars & Clubs

Avenue Pub (p84)

Architecture

Irish Channel (p80)

Shopping

Funky Monkey (p84)

Getting There

🚌 **Bus** No 11 runs along Magazine St from Canal St to Audubon Park.

🚋 **Streetcar** The St Charles Ave streetcar travels through the CBD, the Garden District and Uptown.

Top Sights
Lafayette Cemetery No 1

A thick wall surrounds a battalion of gray crypts at this moody cemetery, a tiny bastion of history, tragedy and Southern Gothic in the heart of the Garden District. It's a place filled with stories – of German and Irish immigrants, yellow fever, social societies doing right by their dead – that pulls the living into New Orleans' long, troubled past. Established in 1833 by the former City of Lafayette, the cemetery is divided by two intersecting footpaths that form a cross.

👁 Map p78, C4

Washington Ave, at Prytania St

admission free

🕑 7am-2:30pm Mon-Fri, to noon Sat

Historic grave stone, Lafayette Cemetery No 1

Don't Miss

Fraternal & Familial Tombs

Look out for the structures built by fraternal organizations such as the Jefferson Fire Company No 22, which took care of its members and their families in large shared crypts. Some of the wealthier family tombs were built of marble, with elaborate detail rivaling the finest architecture in the district, but most tombs were constructed simply of inexpensive plastered brick.

Disease & Disaster

Many who settled close to this area during the early 19th century came as immigrants from overseas. You'll notice many German and Irish names on the above-ground graves, testifying to the fact immigrants were devastated by 19th-century yellow-fever epidemics. Not far from the entrance is a tomb containing the remains of an entire family that died of yellow fever.

Wall Vaults

Wall vaults once surrounded the cemetery, but today they can only be found along Washington Ave. Families were required to wait a year and a day between interring someone into the familial tomb, but diseases such as yellow fever accelerated that timeline; as such, wall vaults had a macabre 'waiting room' utility. Eventually, the vaults became familial tombs themselves.

Notable Graves

Various graves have excellent stories behind them (some of which we may never know in their entirety). Eight women are listed as 'consort' by profession, and there's a French Foreign Legion member buried here. Also, be on the lookout for the 'Secret Garden,' a square of four tombs built by a secret society of friends known as 'The Quarto.'

☑ Top Tips

▶ Visit www.save ourcemeteries.org and www.lafayetteceme tery.org for extensive background on the history of the cemetery.

▶ The New Orleans Public Library (www.nutrias. org) can help you access burial records from 1836 to 1968.

▶ www.lafayette cemetery1.com has a cemetery information database, including photos of individual tombs.

✗ Take a Break

To visit Lafayette Cemetery No 1 and not dine at Commander's Palace (p82) afterwards would be obscene. We don't usually mix fine food with graves, but it's the natural course when two old-school Southern institutions are set so close to each other.

Commander's can get both crowded and expensive, so if you'd like to turn down the price and customer crush, consider the playful, modern Southern cuisine on offer at Coquette (p82).

Local Life
Shopping on Magazine Street

For the true-blue shopper, New Orleans doesn't get much better than leafy Magazine St. For some 6 miles the street courses through the Warehouse District and along the riverside edge of the Garden District and Uptown. It's lined nearly the entire way with shops selling antiques, art, crafts, furniture, jewelry, contemporary fashions, vintage clothing, and other odds and ends.

1 Half Moon

We believe in starting your shopping journey in a locals' dive bar. The **Half Moon** (☎504-522-7313; www.halfmoon grillnola.com; 1125 St Mary St; ⏰5pm-2am) beckons visitors with a cool neighborhood vibe just half a block from Magazine St. It's good for beer, short-order meals, random conversation or shooting stick. Look for the sweet neon sign.

❷ Jim Russell Records

Jim Russell Records (📞504-522-2602; www.jimrussellrecords.com; 1837 Magazine St; ⌚noon-4:30pm Mon-Sat) is a dense emporium of used 45s, with some very rare and collectible disks featuring all the blues, R & B and soul stars of the past. The LPs have mostly given way to CDs, and Russell, a former DJ who opened the store in 1968, died in 2014, but the store rocks on.

❸ Aidan Gill

Shave and a haircut? $40... Apiece. At suave barbershop **Aidan Gill** (📞504-587-9090; www.aidangillformen.com; 2026 Magazine St; ⌚10am-6pm Mon-Fri, 9am-5pm Sat, noon-6pm Sun) it's all about looking neat and stylish, in a leather-and-shoe-polish, masculine sort of way. High-end shaving gear and smart gifts for men are sold in front, and the barber shop is in back.

❹ GoGo Jewelry

If you're looking for stylish jewelry – rings, necklaces, cuffs – with a bit of sass, **GoGo** (www.ilovegogojewelry.com; 2036 Magazine St; ⌚11am-5pm Mon-Sat) is the place to start. Designs are the passion of Janet 'Gogo' Ferguson, who grew up on Cumberland Island, southernmost of the Georgia barrier sea islands. The island's ecology and marine life inspire many of the pieces.

❺ Simon of New Orleans

Local artist Simon Hardeveld has made a name for himself by painting groovy signs that hang like artwork in restaurants all over New Orleans.

You'll probably recognize the distinctive stars, dots and sparkles that fill the spaces between letters. **Simon of New Orleans** (📞504-524-8201; 1028 Jackson Ave; ⌚10am-5pm Mon-Sat) is part of Antiques on Jackson, which Hardeveld owns with his wife Maria.

❻ District: Donuts Sliders Brew

Pit stop! **District** (www.donutsandsliders. com; 2209 Magazine St; doughnuts & pastries under $6, sliders $4-6; ⌚7am-9pm) makes us feel naughty, in a good way. In the morning, truly decadent doughnuts line the counter. Try the piled-high cookies and cream. After 11am, fancy sliders step onto the scene. Fortunately, they're small, so the guilt isn't overwhelming. Note the 'brew' here is coffee, not beer.

❼ Storyville

You may have noticed a trend in clothing shops that sell T-shirts emblazoned with clever, hyper-local slogans aimed at eliciting a smile and nod of recognition from local residents. **Storyville** (www.storyvilleapparel.com; 3029 Magazine St; ⌚10am-8pm) sells these shirts, and you know what? They're damned clever.

❽ New Orleans Music Exchange

Ladies might get a 'Can I help you baby?' when exploring the large **New Orleans Music Exchange** (📞504-891-7670; 3342 Magazine St; ⌚10:30am-6pm Mon-Sat, 1-5pm Sun), which specializes mostly in secondhand instruments. It's the place to go for a nice used horn. There's an entire room of brass and woodwinds, all priced fairly, and a maze of guitars and amps.

9 ⊗ 16

Felicity St

S Liberty St

Oretha Castle-Haley Blvd

◉ 3
Ashé Cultural Arts Center

0
0   500 m
0.25 miles

SimonBolívar St

S Saratoga St

Danneel St

Jackson Ave

For reviews see

◉ Top Sights	p74
◉ Sights	p80
⊗ Eating	p81
● Drinking	p84
☆ Entertainment	p84
⌂ Shopping	p84

Loyola St

Baronne St

2
◉
McKenna Museum of African American Art

Lasalle St

S Liberty St

Lafayette Cemetery No 2

Saratoga St

Philip St

Brainard St

Jackson Ave 🚉

Washington Ave

Danneel St

Second St

First St

Dryades St

Baronne St

Sixth St

Carondelet St

Harmony St

Seventh St

Louisiana Ave

Toledano St

Eighth St

🚉 **Washington Ave**

First St

Second St

Third St

Danneel St

Comery St

Fourth St

Dryades St

Louisiana Ave

St Charles Ave

5
⊗

Lafayette ◉
Cemetery No 1

GARDEN DISTRICT

🚉 **Louisiana**

Harmony St

Eighth St

Seventh St

Sixth St

8
⊗

Delachaise St

Prytania St

Foucher St

Antonine St

Coliseum St

Camp St

18 ⌂

6 ⊗

◉ 1
Irish Channel

Pleasant St

Toledano St

17 ⌂

Magazine St

Constance St

Aline St

Chestnut St

◉ 14

9th St

Harmony St

12 ◉

Laurel St

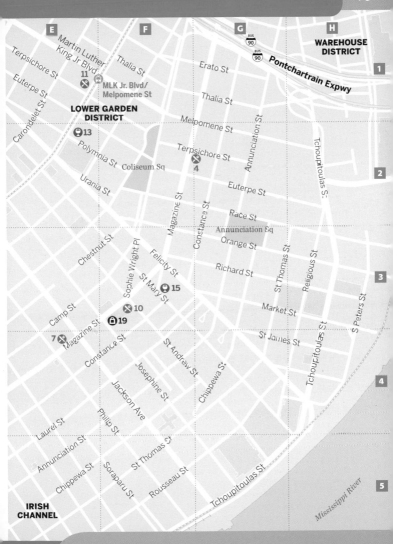

E **F** **G** **H**

WAREHOUSE DISTRICT

Terpsichore St

Martin Luther King Jr Blvd

Thalia St

Erato St

Pontchartrain Expwy

Euterpe St

11

MLK Jr. Blvd/ Melpomene St

Thalia St

Caronlelet St

LOWER GARDEN DISTRICT

Melpomene St

Annunciation St

Tchoupitoulas S.

13

Polymnia St

Coliseum Sq

Terpsichore St

4

Euterpe St

Urania St

Magazine St

Constance St

Race St

Annunciation Sq

Orange St

Chestnut St

Sophie Wright Pl

Felicity St

St Mary St

Richard St

St Thomas St

Religious St

S Peters St

15

Market St

Camp St

10

19

St James St

Tchoupitoulas St

7

Magazine St

Constance St

St Andrew St

Josephine St

Chippewa St

Jackson Ave

Laurel St

Philip St

Annunciation St

Chippewa St

Soraparu St

St Thomas St

Rousseau St

Tchoupitoulas St

Mississippi River

IRISH CHANNEL

1

2

3

4

5

Sights

Irish Channel
NEIGHBORHOOD

1 ◎ Map p78, D5

The name Irish Channel is a bit of a misnomer. Although this historic neighborhood, which borders the Garden District, was settled by poor Irish immigrants fleeing the 1840s potato famine, many German and black residents have coexisted here in a truly multicultural gumbo. This is still a working-class cluster of shotgun houses and you may not want to walk around alone at night, but in general it's pleasant for ambling. Come St Paddy's Day, a big block party takes over Constance St in front of Parasol's.

McKenna Museum of African American Art
MUSEUM

2 ◎ Map p78, D2

Although the displayed work at this beautiful two-story institution comes from all over the African diaspora, most of it is created by local New Orleans artists. Images of Mardi Gras and the New Orleans music scene are highlights. The artwork is part of a collection amassed during some 30 years of collecting by Dr Dwight McKenna. Real standouts are the temporary exhibitions, such as 2014's *Queens Rule!*, a celebration of Mardi Gras Indian queens. Check the website for details of the packed calendar. (📞504-586-7432; www.themckennamuseum.com; 2003 Carondelet St; adult/students & seniors $5/3; ⊗11am-4pm Thu-Sat, by appointment Tue & Wed)

Understand
The History of Lafayette Cemetery No 1

'It was a victim of its own popularity' is a sentiment not often expressed around interment areas, but Lafayette Cemetery No 1 (p74) isn't any old cemetery. The quintessential Gothic graveyard filled to capacity within decades of its opening – more than 10,000 people are buried here.

All this happened before the surrounding neighborhood reached peak affluence. As such, many of the plots at Lafayette No 1 have occupants of humbler means than the surrounding streetscape might imply. And when Mid-City's prestigious Metairie Cemetery opened in 1872, its opulent grounds appealed to those with truly extravagant and flamboyant tastes.

But the odd energy that surrounds the atmospheric Lafayette Cemetery No 1 was bound to be discovered by future generations. In July 1995 author Anne Rice staged her own funeral here. She hired a horse-drawn hearse and a brass band to play dirges, and wore an antique wedding dress as she laid down in a coffin. The event coincided with the release of one of her novels.

KYLIE MCLAUGHLIN/GETTY IMAGES ©

Classic historic home, Garden District

Ashé Cultural Arts Center

ARTS CENTER

3 Map p78, D1

An important anchor for the local African American community, Ashé (from a Yoruba word that could loosely be translated as 'Amen') regularly showcases performances, art and photography exhibitions, movie screenings and lectures with an African, African American or Caribbean focus, and beyond. Check the online calendar for upcoming events. The on-site **Diaspora Boutique** (⊗10am-6pm Mon-Sat), which stocks clothing, earrings and crafts, is also worth a look. (☏504-569-9070; www.ashecac.org; 1712 Oretha Castle-Haley Blvd)

Eating

Surrey's Juice Bar

AMERICAN $

4 ✖ Map p78, G2

Surrey's makes a simple bacon-and-egg sandwich taste – and look – like the most delicious breakfast you've ever been served. And you know what? It probably *is* the best. Boudin biscuits; eggs scrambled with salmon; biscuits swimming in salty sausage gravy; and a shrimp, grits and bacon dish that should be illegal. And the juice, as you might guess, is blessedly fresh. Cash only. (☏504-524-3828; 1418 Magazine St; breakfast & lunch $6-13; ⊗8am-3pm)

Local Life

Southern Food & Beverage Museum

This **museum** (☎504-569-0405; www. southernfood.org; 1504 Oretha Castle-Haley Blvd; adult/child under 12yr $10/ free; ⊙11am-5:30pm Thu-Mon) celebrates Southern foodways and cocktails with exhibits sourced from every state south of the Mason-Dixon. The well-stocked Museum of the American Cocktail displays old elixir bottles, cocktail-making tools, and a picture of an impressively mustachioed bartender. In the back corner, La Galerie Absinthe re-creates the 1895 Old Absinthe House. Check the website for details about cooking classes.

Commander's Palace CREOLE $$$

5 Map p78, C4

Commander's Palace is a dapper host, a seer-suckered bon vivant who wows with white-linen dining rooms, decadent dishes and attentive Southern hospitality. The nouveau Creole menu runs from crispy oysters with brie-cauliflower fondue to shrimp and grits with goat's cheese and roasted mushrooms. The dress code adds to the charm – no shorts or T-shirts; jackets preferred at dinner. It's a *very* nice place – but also lots of fun. (☎504-899-8221; www.commanderspalace.com; 1403 Washington Ave; dinner mains $28-45; ⊙6:30-10:30pm daily, 11:30am-2pm Mon-Fri, 11:30am-1pm Sat, 10:30am-1:30pm Sun)

Coquette MODERN FRENCH $$

6 Map p78, D5

Coquette mixes wine-bar ambience with friendly service and a bit of white linen; the result is a candle-lit place where you don't feel bad getting tipsy. Explore beyond the respectable wine menu, though – there's some great Louisiana-sourced food here, often with an innovative global spin. Choices may include crawfish bisque with oyster cream and truffle, or a succulent red snapper with ham hock broth. (☎504-265-0421; www.coquettenola.com; 2800 Magazine St; small plates lunch $11-22, dinner $12-24, mains lunch $16-23, dinner $24-32; ⊙11:30am-2:30pm Fri & Sat, 10:30am-2pm Sun, 5:30-10pm daily)

Stein's Deli DELI $

7 Map p78, E4

You may get a no-nonsense 'What?' when you step up to the counter, but it's just part of the schtick at this scruffy deli. For quality sandwiches, cheese and cold cuts, this is as good as the city gets. Owner Dan Stein is a fanatic about keeping his deli stocked with great Italian and Jewish meats and cheeses, and some fine boutique beers. (☎504-527-0771; www.steinsdeli.net; 2207 Magazine St; sandwiches $7-13; ⊙7am-7pm Tue-Fri, 9am-5pm Sat & Sun)

Parasol's SANDWICHES $

8 Map p78, D4

Parasol's isn't just in the Irish Channel; it sort of *is* the Irish Channel, serving as community center, nexus of gossip and, naturally, watering hole. Yes, it's first and foremost a bar, but you can order some of the best po'boys in town from the seating area in the back. That big ol' roast beef is a messy, juice-filled conduit of deliciousness. (☎504 302-1533; www.parasolsbarandrestaurant.com; 2533 Constance St; po'boys $7-16; ☺11am-9pm Sun-Thu, to 10pm Fri & Sat)

Café Reconcile DINER $

 9 Map p78, D1

Café Reconcile fights the good fight by recruiting and training at-risk youth to work as kitchen and floor staff. The food is simple and, frankly, really good. It's very much of the humble New Orleans school of home cookery: red beans and rice, fried chicken, shrimp Creole and the like, with the spotlight on daily specials. (☎504-568-1157; www.reconcileneworleans.org; 1631 Oretha Castle-Haley Blvd; mains $9-15; ☺11am-2:30pm Mon-Fri)

Juan's Flying Burrito MEXICAN $

10 Map p78, F3

The answer to that perennial question, 'What happens when you cross a bunch of skinny-jeans-clad hipsters with a tortilla?' is (ta-da) Juan's. The food is about as authentically Mexican as Ontario, but that doesn't mean it's not good; the hefty burritos pack a satisfying punch. The margaritas are tasty and the quesadilla comes with ground beef, bacon and blue cheese –

yes, please. (☎504-569-0000; www.juansflyingburrito.com; 2018 Magazine St; mains $5-14; ☺11am-10pm Sun-Thu, to 11pm Fri & Sat)

Slice PIZZA $

11 Map p78, E1

One of those places you'll find yourself returning to again and again if you're staying in the Lower Garden District for more than a few days. Highlights? Nice staff, happy-hour specials (2pm to 6pm) and damn good pizza. Toppings for the thin-crust pies can be as artisanal or run-of-the-mill as you like. Slices start at $3. Also serves po'boys, pastas and salads. (☎504-525-7437; www.slicepizzeria.com; 1513 St Charles Ave; mains $8-13, pizzas $13-22; ☺11am-11pm Mon-Sat, to 10pm Sun)

Local Life
House of Broel

The 1850s **House of Broel** (☎504-522-2220; www.houseofbroel.com; 2220 St Charles Ave; adult/child under 12yr $10/5; ☺tours 11am-3pm Mon-Fri) is an excellent example of a Garden District mansion, an oddly enormous museum of dolls, and a function hall for those who grow up on this leafy end of Orleans Parish. Consider a tour: you can see a *Best Little Whorehouse in Texas* doll diorama that includes a lady of the night on a teeny tiny bed.

Drinking

NOLA Brewing
BREWERY

12 Map p78, D5

Free craft beer at 2pm on Fridays. Yep, you read right. This cavernous brewery welcomes guests once a week for a free brewery tour that kicks off with sloshy cups of craft brew, and a food truck or two out front. The rest of the week? Stop by the cozy taproom where 16 beers await. (☑504-301-1117; www.nolabrewing.com; 3001 Tchoupitoulas St; ⏱2-11pm Mon-Thu, 1-11pm Fri, 11am-11:30pm Sat & Sun)

Avenue Pub
PUB

13 Map p78, E2

From the street, this scruffy pub looks like a nothing-special neighborhood dive. But with more than 40 beers on tap and another 135-odd in bottles, plus a staff with serious dedication to the taste of their drafts, this two-story beer bar is earning national accolades. The bourbon list is impressive, too. The upstairs patio is a fine place to watch the world go by. (www.theavenuepub.com; 1732 St Charles Ave; ⏱24hr)

Bulldog
BAR

14 Map p78, C5

With 40 or so brews on tap and more than 100 by the bottle or can – from Louisiana to Mexico to Italy and points beyond – the Bulldog works hard to keep beer enthusiasts happy. The best place to sink a pint is in the courtyard, which gets packed with the young and beautiful almost every evening when the weather is warm. (☑504-891-1516; www.draftfreak.com; 3236 Magazine St; ⏱11:30am-2am Mon-Fri, 11am-2am Sat & Sun)

Saint Bar & Lounge
BAR

15 Map p78, F3

The Saint? Of what? How about a great backyard beer garden enclosed in duck blinds and filled with tattooed young professionals, Tulane students, good shots, good beers, good times and a photo booth that you will inevitably end up in before the night is through. It's not the cleanest bar (nickname: the Taint), but it sure is a fun one. (☑504-523-0500; www.thesaintneworleans.com; 961 St Mary St; ⏱7pm-late)

Entertainment

Zeitgeist
CINEMA

16 Map p78, D1

This old movie house has been around since the 1920s. It screens independent and art films. (☑504-352-1150; www.zeitgeistnola.org; 1618 Oretha Castle-Haley Blvd; adult/concession $8/7)

Shopping

Funky Monkey
VINTAGE

17 Map p78, C5

You'll find wigs in every color at Funky Monkey, which sells vintage attire for club-hopping men and women. This funhouse of frippery is also a good

Funky Monkey, Magazine St

spot for Mardi Gras costumes. It's tiny, though, and can get jam-packed with customers. In addition to wigs, look for jeans, jewelry, tops, sunglasses, hats and boots. (☏504-899-5587; www.facebook.com/funkymonkeyneworleans; 3127 Magazine St; ☺11am-6pm Mon-Wed, to 7pm Thu-Sat, noon-6pm Sun)

Magazine Antique Mall ANTIQUES

18 🔒 Map p78, C5

Scary baby dolls. Hats. Chandeliers. Coca-Cola memorabilia. Inside this overstuffed emporium, rummagers are likely to score items of interest in the dozen or so stalls, where independent dealers peddle an intriguing and varied range of antique bric-a-brac. Bargain hunters aren't likely to have much luck, though. (☏504-896-9994; www.magazineantiquemall.com; 3017 Magazine St; ☺10:30am-5:30pm, from noon Sun)

Trashy Diva CLOTHING

19 🔒 Map p78, F3

It isn't really as scandalous as the name suggests, except by Victorian standards. Diva's specialty is sassy 1940s- and '50s-style cinched, hourglass dresses and belle epoque undergarments – lots of corsets, lace and such. The shop also features Kabuki-inspired dresses with embroidered dragons, and retro tops, skirts and shawls reflecting styles plucked from just about every era. (☏504-299-8777; www.trashydiva.com; 2048 Magazine St; ☺noon-6pm Mon-Fri, 11am-6pm Sat, 1-5pm Sun)

Explore

Uptown & Audubon

Green and leafy Uptown is one of the wealthiest residential neighborhoods in New Orleans, but that hardly means it's sleepy. You'll find bars and restaurants clustered around the ever-lively strip of Magazine St, with many patrons drawn from nearby Tulane and Loyola Universities. Gorgeous Audubon Park, home of the fascinating Audubon Zoo, bisects much of the neighborhood.

The Sights in a Day

Start with coffee on Magazine St, and then head for the **Audubon Zoo** (p90). It's on the grounds of **Audubon Park** (p92), so when you're done there, head into the park and walk towards the campus of Tulane University while enjoying the live oaks along the way.

Now that you're at Tulane, walk east along Freret St into a rapidly gentrifying business corridor filled with good bars and excellent restaurants. We suggest getting lunch at **Dat Dog** (p98). When you've finished snacking, do some Freret St window-shopping, then grab a cab or dive back to Magazine St.

As the evening sets in, book yourself a romantic dinner at **Gautreau's** (p96). If you're feeling a little more casual about supper, grab a po'boy instead at **Mahony's** (p96). Finish the day with drinks at **St Joe's** (p99) and some live music at **Tipitina's** (p100).

For a local's day in Audubon Park, see p92.

👁 Top Sights

St Charles Avenue Streetcar (p88)

Audubon Zoological Gardens (p90)

🔍 Local Life

Audubon Park & Around (p92)

❤ Best of New Orleans

Eating
Mahony's Po-Boy Shop (p96)

Domilise's Po-Boys (p98)

Gautreau's (p96)

Live Music
Freret Street Publiq House (p99)

Tipitina's (p100)

With Kids
Audubon Zoo (p90)

Audubon Park (p92)

Getting There

🚌 **Bus** No 11 runs along Magazine St from Canal St to Audubon Park.

🚋 **Streetcar** The St Charles Ave streetcar travels through the CBD, the Garden District and Uptown.

🚗 **Car** Metered parking ($1.50 per hour) is required along much of Magazine St from 8am to 6pm Monday to Saturday. Look for free parking on side streets.

Top Sights
St Charles Avenue Streetcar

A buck twenty-five gets you on the St Charles Ave streetcar, which plies the oldest continuously operating street railway system in the world. New Orleanians are justifiably proud of this moving monument, which began life as the nation's second horse-drawn streetcar line, the New Orleans & Carrollton Railroad, in 1835. In 1893 the line was among the first systems to be electrified. Now it is one of the few streetcars in the USA to have survived the automobile era.

👁 Map p94, E3

per ride $1.25

Don't Miss

Tree-mendous

It's only slightly hyperbolic to claim St Charles Ave is the most beautiful street in the country. Almost the entire length is shrouded under a tunnel of Southern live oak trees. These massive specimens, whose roots have overgrown local sidewalks and whose shade arches over the entire street, were planted during the early 20th century.

Villa Views

Gorgeous homes that house the aristocratic elite of the city are lined up and down St Charles Ave. Many of the residents of these homes ride in the floats that proceed along St Charles during Carnival season; look up to the tree branches and you'll see many are laden with shiny beads tossed from Mardi Gras floats.

Neutral Territory

Within the Neutral Ground – the median that houses the streetcar tracks – you'll often see joggers and families passing through the verdant corridor of live oaks. You'll also see turning cars that hold up the streetcar – the interplay of motor traffic and streetcar route is part of the reason this form of public transportation is rare in the USA.

More Streetcar!

Have you ridden the streetcar and been like, 'Man, I need some more streetcar?' We feel you, public-transportation aficionado, and have good news: the St Charles streetcar connects with the Canal St streetcar, which has two lines – City Park, which ends at (guess!) City Park, and the ominous-sounding Cemeteries, which ends at Greenwood Cemeteries. A transfer costs 25¢.

☑ **Top Tips**

▶ You may want to invest in a Jazzy Pass, which has a silly name but gives you unlimited rides on streetcars and buses for one ($3) or three ($9) days. Jazzy Passes can be bought online at www.norta. com, or you can buy a one-day pass from a streetcar operator.

▶ Streetcars are scheduled to arrive every 15 minutes, 24 hours a day. The 24 hours part is true; every 15 minutes is a little optimistic, but it's close.

✕ **Take a Break**

Walk to Magazine St and Mahony's (p96) for a po'boy.

Fancy a fancy drink? Head to the Columns Hotel (p100) for a cocktail with a side of Southern gentility.

Top Sights
Audubon Zoological Gardens

The gray foxes sleeping on the rocking chairs in the Louisiana Swamp exhibit clearly have this zoo thing figured out. And they don't seem too worried about the alligators loitering around the bend. The Louisiana Swamp is one of ten animal exhibit areas at the Audubon Zoo, which is home to an excellent array of international animals, from Asian elephants and Komodo dragons to towering giraffes and a poisonous dart frog or two, all scattered across thoughtfully landscaped grounds.

👁 Map p94, B4

☎ 504-581-4629

www.auduboninstitute.org

6500 Magazine St

adult/child 2-12yr $19/14

🕑 10am-4pm Tue-Fri, to 5pm Sat & Sun Sep-Feb, 10am-5pm Mon-Fri, to 6pm Sat & Sun Mar-Aug

Flamingos, Audubon Zoological Gardens

Don't Miss

Jaguar Temple & Pampas

A memorable section of the zoo is a South American corner that includes the Mayan-style Jaguar Jungle and the South America Pampas with its raised walkway. Poems and quotes, from Emily Dickinson to Langston Hughes, dot the walkways and add atmosphere while eco-minded plaques reinforce the precarious position of many of the animals in the wild.

Louisiana Swamp

This engaging Cajun setting explores life in the bayou. An authentic fishing camp displays shrimp trawls, crawfish traps and an oyster dredge. Bobcats and lynx are also on view, and you may see a red fox chilling on a log in the swamp scrub. Human intrusions are poignantly represented by a Traânasee cutter, used by fish and game trappers.

Reptile Encounter

Louisiana, land of gators, has a thing for scaly creatures, as evidenced by this excellent reptile house. It's the sort of place that draws in folks who tend to shirk from lizards and snakes. Displays include a beefy Komodo dragon and some of the largest snakes in the world – from the king cobra to the green anaconda.

Watoto Walk

The child-focused Watoto Walk, built to resemble Masai villages in Kenya and Tanzania, is a petting zoo that integrates biology and anthropology education. With that said, the well thought out African theme merely sets the scene, and doesn't extend to the wildlife; your kids aren't going to pet lions. Rather, the 3000-sq-ft enclosure houses goats and sheep.

JUDY BELLAH/GETTY IMAGES ©

☑ Top Tips

▶ The zoo is least crowded on weekday afternoons. On weekends, it can be, well, a zoo.

▶ Ask about 'Wild Walks' if you'd like a personalized tour of the zoo.

▶ During the summer, the kid-focused 'Cool Zoo' water park opens at the zoo.

▶ Strollers are allowed inside the zoo, and can be rented.

▶ Buy tickets online to avoid real lines.

✕ Take a Break

Repair to the wonderful Clancy's (p96) for lunch (Thursdays and Fridays) or visit the zoo in the afternoon and head there afterwards for an early dinner.

Take a stroll away from the park to enjoy a beer on the patio of the inimitable St Joe's (p99) bar.

Local Life
Audubon Park & Around

Audubon Park is a grand green space, run through with live oak trees, walking and cycling paths and picturesque waterways, all framed by some of the city's grandest residences. Students and locals lounge on the grass under hairy tendrils of Spanish moss, or jog, play with their pets, or have an outdoor sundowner. Basically, it's an emerald, urban idyll.

❶ Big Branches

Start your walk near the bottom of **Audubon Park** (⏰5am-10pm), where the first landmark is the largest tree in the park: the Etienne de Boré Oak, or Tree of Life. This plant boasts a massive girth of 35ft and a leaf crown more than 160ft wide. Families bring kids here to climb the low-hanging, splayed-out branches.

2 Oak Allee

Oak Allee runs below Magazine St into the northern half of Audubon Park. It's a beautiful, veritable hallway of live oaks, and a favorite spot for dog-walkers and those taking early-evening lovers' strolls. Near the southern half of the 'allee,' you may smell the scent of horses housed at Cascade Stables.

3 Happy Trails

A nature trail runs around the entire northern half of the park. At the intersection of the trail and Prytania St, you'll find the muddy waters of Olmsted 'Lake.' Local couples sometimes cuddle near the Newman Bandstand, while those seeking quiet wander around the WWI monument and garden.

4 Tulane University

The campus of **Tulane** (504-865-5000; www.tulane.edu; 6823 St Charles Ave), a premier Southern university, is a pleasant spot for wandering. The grounds are an attractive tableau of live oaks, red-brick buildings and green quads spread across 110 acres above Audubon Park. Tulane boasts big-name alumni including Jacques Chirac and a long list of Louisiana governors, judges and politicos.

5 A Jazz Journey

Local music geeks can often be found at the **Hogan Jazz Archive** (504-865-5688; http://jazz.tulane.edu; 3rd fl, Jones Hall, 6801 Freret St, Tulane University; 8:30am-5:30pm Mon-Fri), where oral histories form the heart of the holdings. This collection of New Orleans jazz artifacts includes sheet music, photographs, journals and recordings. Most of the archive's wealth of material is not exhibited but the helpful staff will retrieve items.

6 Art Museum

Flanked by beautiful Tiffany stained-glass triptychs, the **Newcomb Art Gallery** (504-865-5328; www.newcombartgallery.tulane.edu; 6823 St Charles Ave, Woldenberg Art Center; admission free; 10am-5pm Tue-Fri, 11am-4pm Sat & Sun) is a great spot to soak up art, typically with a local or regional spin. You'll often find Uptowners and students here enjoying the quiet, contemplative atmosphere. Just outside is a pretty green where kids sunbathe, toss Frisbees and recede into the happiest rhythms of American higher ed.

7 Golf & Mansions

Now re-enter Audubon Park from the northwest. As the trail loops around the west end of the park and heads south to Magazine St, it runs adjacent to Walnut St and some of the city's most beautiful (and as you may surmise, expensive) homes. The center of the park is taken up by the Audubon Park Golf Course.

8 The Fly

Walk south from Magazine St for half a mile to reach the Fly, an elevated (for New Orleans) area that overlooks the Mississippi River. It's one of the most popular picnic spots in the city, and on nice days you'll see families enjoying a beer while children log-roll down the artificial hills.

A | B | C | D

1

Pearl St
Dominican St
Benjamin St
Hurst St
Garfield St
Leake Ave
Lowerline St
Pine St
Broadway
St Charles Ave

Tulane University

Loyola University

Tulane University/ Audubon Park & Zoo

Loyola St

Calhoun St

Palmer Ave

2

Pitt St
Prytania St
Broadway St
Audubon St
Walnut St

Loyola University

Exposition Blvd
Benjamin St
Hurst St
Garfield St
Pitt St
Prytania St
Perrier St
Coliseum St

3

Mississippi River

Audubon Park Trail

Audubon Park Golf Course

Audubon Park

Magazine St

Calhoun St
Henry Clay Ave
Webster St

Chestnut St
Camp St
Magazine St
Constance St
Patton St

4

Riverview Dr

East Dr

Audubon Zoological Gardens

Laurel St
Annunciation St
Tchoupitoulas St
State St

9

4

Eleonore Ave
Nashville Ave
Arabella St

For reviews see

⊙	Top Sights	p88
⊙	Sights	p96
⊗	Eating	p96
⊙	Drinking	p99
☆	Entertainment	p100
🔒	Shopping	p101

N

0 ————————— 1 km
0 ————————— 0.5 miles

E F G H

Willow St
Clara St
Clara St

State St
Joseph St
Octavia St
Jefferson Ave

Magnolia St
S Robertson St
Gen Taylor St
Marengo St
Gen Pershing St

1

Nashville Ave

12
Freret St
7 **16 18**
La Salle St
S Liberty St

S Robertson St
Jena St
Cadiz St
11
Napoleon Ave
Milan St

Valence St

Loyola St

2

Saratoga St
Danneel St
Dryades St
Baronne St
Carondelet St

Arrella St
Peniston St

Nashville
2
Saratoga St
Upperline St

**St Charles
Avenue
Streetcar**

Jefferson Ave

14
8

3

Milton Latter
Memorial Library **1**

St Charles Ave
Napoleon
Pitt St
Prytania St

Pitt St

17

Perrier St
Coliseum St
Chestnut St
Camp St

Gen Pershing St
Milan St
Marengo St
Constantinople St

4

Joseph St
Octavia St
Leontine St
Valmont St

Jefferson Ave

Dufossat St
Soniat St
Robert St
Upperline St

13

UPTOWN

Napoleon Ave
Jena St
Cadiz St
Valence St

19
Magazine St
3
Constance St

10

5

Bellecastle St

Lyons St
Borceaux St

Laurel St
Annunciation St

Laurel St
Annunciation St

15

6

Tchoupitoulas St

5

Sights

Milton Latter
Memorial Library   BUILDING

1 ◎ Map p94, F3

Poised elegantly above shady stands
of palms, the Latter Memorial Library
was once a private mansion. The
Isaac family (owners 1907–12) –
who installed Flemish-style carved
woodwork, Dutch murals and French
frescoed ceilings – passed the property
to aviator Harry Williams and his
silent-film-star wife, Marguerite Clark
(1912–39). The couple was known
for throwing grand parties. The next
owner was local horse racer Robert S
Eddy, followed by Mr and Mrs Harry
Latter, who gave the building to the
city in 1948. (☑504-596-2625; www.
neworleanspubliclibrary.org; 5120 St Charles
Ave; ⊙9am-8pm Mon & Wed, to 6pm Tue &
Thu, 10am-5pm Sat, noon-5pm Sun)

Eating

Gautreau's   MODERN AMERICAN $$$

2 🍴 Map p94, F3

There's no sign outside Gautreau's,
just the number 1728 discreetly mark-
ing a nondescript house in a residential neighborhood. Cross the threshold
to find a refined but welcoming dining
room where savvy diners, many of
them New Orleanian food aficionados,
dine on fresh, modern American fare.
Chef Sue Zemanick has won every
award a rising young star can garner

in American culinary circles. (☑504-
899-7397; www.gautreausrestaurant.com;
1728 Soniat St; mains $22-42; ⊙6-10pm
Mon-Sat)

Mahony's Po-Boy
Shop   SANDWICHES $

3 🍴 Map p94, H4

A convenient po'boy place with a fun
atmosphere, Mahony's is a welcome if
sometimes expensive choice. Digs are
a converted Magazine St house with a
tiny front porch. The Peacemaker with
fried oysters, bacon and cheddar is a
crowd-pleaser as is the grilled shrimp
and fried green tomatoes, although we
found the latter, at $14.95, lacking in
oomph. (www.mahonyspoboys.com; 3454
Magazine St; po'boys $9-22; ⊙11am-9pm)

Clancy's   CREOLE $$$

4 🍴 Map p94, C5

This white-tablecloth neighborhood
restaurant embraces style, the good
life and Creole cuisine with a chatter-
ing *joie de vivre* and top-notch service.
The city's professional set comes here
to gossip and savor the specialties:
fried oysters and brie, veal with crab-
meat and béarnaise, and lobster and
mushroom risotto. Want to go where
the locals go? Come here, and dress up
a little. Reservations recommended.
(☑504-895-1111; www.clancysneworleans.
com; 6100 Annunciation St; mains lunch $16-
18, dinner $25-35; ⊙11:30am-2pm Thu & Fri,
5:30-10:30pm Mon-Sat)

Understand

Making the Most of Mardi Gras

-- -- -- -- -- -- -- -- -- -- -- -- -- -- -- -- -- --

Mardi Gras is the iconic New Orleans holiday, and much of it centers on Uptown. The most popular parade route, the St Charles Ave route, starts at Jefferson Ave and Magazine St, and proceeds up Napoleon Ave, at the edge of Uptown, to St Charles.

It's important to understand that Mardi Gras is more a culmination of a season (Carnival season) than a singular holiday. The parade season is a 12-day period beginning two Fridays before Fat Tuesday (Mardi Gras). Early parades are charming, neighborly processions of local Mardi Gras 'krewes'; these processions whet your appetite for the later parades, which increase in size and grandeur as Fat Tuesday approaches.

Each parade is known for its 'throws' – baubles tossed from a float to the crowd. With the exception of the French Quarter on Mardi Gras day, the Carnival season is by and large a family-oriented affair and, despite popular myth, locals keep their clothes on. A favorite Uptown krewe is Muses, an all-women's krewe that showcases imaginative, innovative floats; their throws include much-coveted hand-decorated shoes.

On Mardi Gras morning, the krewes of Zulu and Rex, representing the elite of African American and white New Orleans, parade along the St Charles route. Zulu members distribute their prized hand-painted coconuts, while the 'King of Carnival,' Rex, waits further Uptown; his parade is a much more restrained affair.

Costume Up!

Mardi Gras is a citywide costume party, and many locals take a dim view of visitors who crash the party without one. For truly fantastic outfits, march with the Society of St Ann on Mardi Gras morning. This collection of artists and misfits prides itself on its DIY outfits, which seem to have marched out of a collision between a David Bowie video and a '60s acid trip. The creativity and pageantry on display really needs to be seen to be believed.

Learn More

Gambit Weekly (www.bestofneworleans.com) publishes a Carnival edition during February or March, depending on the date of Mardi Gras. **Mardi Gras New Orleans** (www.mardigrasneworleans.com) is an excellent website.

Guy's
SANDWICHES $

5 Map p94, E4

It's very simple: Guy's is basically a one-man operation that does some of the best po'boys in town. Sandwiches are made fresh and to order, with a level of attention you don't get anywhere else in the city. Even when the line is out the door – and it often is – each po'boy is painstakingly crafted. (📞504-891-5025; 5259 Magazine St; po'boys $7-13; ⏰11am-4pm Mon-Sat)

Domilise's Po-Boys
CREOLE $

6 Map p94, E5

Domilise's is everything that makes New Orleans great: a dilapidated white shack by the river serving Dixie beer, staffed by long-timers and prepping some of the best po'boys in the city. Locals tell us to opt for the half-and-half (oysters and shrimp) with gravy and cheese, but honestly, we think the oyster, dressed but otherwise on its own, is the height of the po'boy maker's craft. (5240 Annunciation St; po'boys $6-18; ⏰10am-7pm Mon-Wed & Fri, 10:30am-7pm Sat)

> ### Understand
> ### Freret Street Fracas
>
> The 2014 PBS documentary *Getting Back to Abnormal* examines the particularly ugly nature of the Freret district's 2010 city-council race, spotlighting council member Stacy Head, her opponent, race relations and post-Katrina politics.

Dat Dog
AMERICAN $

7 Map p94, F2

Who dat who say Dat Dog? Da whole doggone city, dat's who. Every part of your tasty dog, from the steamed link to the toasted sourdough bun to the flavor-packed toppings, is produced with exuberance. Sausage choices include duck, alligator and crawfish. If you like your dawgs spicy, try the Louisiana hot sausage from nearby Harahan. And grab about 10 napkins for every topping. (📞504-899-6883; www.datdognola.com; 5030 Freret St; mains under $8; ⏰11am-10pm Mon-Sat, to 9pm Sun; 🚴)

Delachaise
INTERNATIONAL $$

8 Map p94, H3

If you're looking for a place to relax, sip wine and watch the world go by, Delachaise is a great choice. It's just steps from the St Charles streetcar line. The small plates are wonderful in their indulgent way, especially the ridiculously over-the-top grilled cheese sandwich with housemade apple butter. And everyone lovingly recalls the *pommes frites* – fried in goose fat. (📞504-895-0858; www.thedelachaise.com; 3442 St Charles Ave; small plates $8-28, cheese plates $13-28; ⏰5pm-late Mon-Thu, 3pm-late Fri-Sun)

Patois
FRENCH, CREOLE $$$

9 Map p94, C5

The interior of Patois feels like the cozy house of very good friends – who happen to be very good cooks. Head chef Aaron Burgau went through his paces in New Orleans' top restaurants, including Commander's Palace, before opening Patois. The setting has an unaffected rustic romantic vibe, while the menu is French haute with New Orleans accents (or 'patois'). (☏504-895-9441; www.patoisnola.com; 6078 Laurel St; brunch $13-19, lunch $13-21, dinner $23-32; ◷5:30-10pm Wed & Thu, to 10:30pm Fri & Sat, 11:30am-2pm Fri, 10:30am-2pm Sun)

Drinking

St Joe's

BAR

10 ⊕ Map p94, E4

The bartender might make a face when you order a blueberry mojito – mojitos are hard to make. But dang, dude, you make 'em so good. They've been voted the best in town by New Orleanians several times. Patrons at this dark-but-inviting place are in their 20s and 30s, and friendly and chatty, as are the staff. (www.stjoesbar.com; 5535 Magazine St; ◷4pm-3am Mon-Fri, noon-3am Sat, to 1am Sun)

Freret Street Publiq House

BAR

11 ⊕ Map p94, G2

Hello Publiq House. Welcome to Freret St. So glad you're here. Let's call this place an *uber*-neighborhood bar – it goes above and beyond your typical corner dive. Trivia night. Cornhole night. Burlesque shows.

Crawfish boils. More than 90 local and national beers available, plus some fancy cocktails. Live music, on a side-room stage, ranges from jazz to rock to funk. (☏504-826-9912; www.publiqhouse.com; 4528 Freret St; ◷4pm-midnight Mon-Thu, 4pm-2am Fri, 2pm-2am Sat, 2pm-midnight Sun; 🐾)

Cure

BAR

12 ⊕ Map p94, F1

This stylish purveyor of cocktails and spirits flickers like an ultramodern apothecary shop, a place where mysterious elixirs are expertly mixed to soothe whatever ails you. A smooth and polished space of modern banquettes, anatomic art and a Zen-garden outdoor area, Cure is where you come for a well-mixed drink, period. It's drinks for adults in a stylish setting. (☏504-302-2357; www.curenola.com; 4905 Freret St; ◷5pm-midnight Sun-Thu, to 2am Fri & Sat)

Le Bon Temps Roulé
BAR

13 🚇 Map p94, F4

A neighborhood bar – a very good one at that – with a mostly college and postcollege crowd drawn in by two pool tables and a commendable beer selection. Late at night, high-caliber blues, zydeco or jazz rocks the joint's little back room. (📞504-897-3448; 4801 Magazine St; ⏲11am-3am)

Columns Hotel
BAR

14 🚇 Map p94, H3

With its antebellum trappings – a raised front porch, white Doric columns, a flanking live oak – the Columns Hotel harks back to a simpler era. Oh yes, we're going to party like it's 1859. But truthfully, it's not as aristocratic as all that; it's more a place where college students and just-graduates act the part of the Southern upper-crust. (www.thecolumns.com; 3811 St Charles Ave; ⏲2pm-midnight Mon-Thu, 11am-2am Fri & Sat, to midnight Sun)

Entertainment

Tipitina's
LIVE MUSIC

15 ⭐ Map p94, H5

'Tips,' as locals call it, is one of New Orleans' great musical meccas. The legendary Uptown nightclub, which takes its name from Professor Longhair's 1953 hit single, is the site of some of the city's most memorable shows, particularly when big names such as Dr John come home to roost. Outstanding music from local talent packs 'em in year-round. (📞504-895-8477; www.tipitinas.com; 501 Napoleon Ave)

Gasa Gasa
LIVE MUSIC

16 ⭐ Map p94, F2

We're unsure what is most interesting at this newish performance and drinking space inside an art gallery: the art, the music or the patrons. The name means 'easily distracted' or 'doing too many things at once' in Japanese – but we can't confirm that because, well, all of the above. Come for an eclectic array of live music, from jazz to folk to indie. Big Freedia was on the lineup for the one-year anniversary. (📞504-304-7110; www.gasagasa.com; 4920 Freret St)

Prytania Theatre
CINEMA

17 ⭐ Map p94, E3

If you're in the mood for a quiet movie, we suggest coming by this single-screen gem. This old movie house has been around since the 1920s, and screens independent and art films as well as classics. Our favorite theater in the city. (📞504-891-2787; www.prytaniatheatreneworleans.com; 5339 Prytania St; tickets adult/child under 12yr/senior $11.50/9.50/9.50, matinee $5.75)

RICHARD CUMMINS/GETTY IMAGES ©

Beads for sale for Mardi Gras festivities, Magazine St

Shopping

Crescent City Comics COMICS

18 🔒 Map p94, F2

Helpful, on-the-ball staff members are what make Crescent City Comics shine. The store is compact but well stocked, with sections dedicated to everything from local comics to underground to graphic reads. Neil Gaiman and sci-fi action figures are also in the stacks. Check it out. (www.crescentcitycomics.com; 4916 Freret St; ⏱11am-7pm Mon-Sat, noon-6pm Sun)

Uptown Costume & Dancewear CLOTHING

19 🔒 Map p94, H4

A one stop emergency shop for anyone caught completely unprepared for Mardi Gras, Halloween or any other occasion that calls for a disguise. It's an emporium of goofy get-ups, packed with boas, masks, Elvis capes, ballerina tutus and a truly astounding selection of cheap-ass wigs. Guaranteed to keep you from blending into the woodwork, and fun stuff for the entire family. (☎504-895-7969; 4326 Magazine St; ⏱11am-6pm Mon-Wed, to 7pm Thu & Fri, 10am-6pm Sat)

Local Life
Exploring the Riverbend

Getting There

The Riverbend can be accessed by Carrollton Ave from Mid-City.

Take the St Charles Ave streetcar from Uptown.

The Levee Path is a natural neighborhood cycling thoroughfare.

The Riverbend, also known as Carrollton, sits at the juncture of the Mississippi River and Orleans and Jefferson Parishes. It's a lush slice of tree-lined New Orleans, not as posh as adjacent Uptown, nor as family-oriented as nearby Mid-City. Proximity to Tulane and Loyola Universities makes for a studenty atmosphere, which manifests in plenty of cafes, restaurants, bars and shops.

1 Levee Path

This public greenway runs atop the levee and follows the curves of the Mississippi River from the Fly (p93) behind Audubon Park to Jefferson Parish and beyond. It's a nice spot for walking, jogging or cycling.

2 Cooter Brown's

Head off the levee near where Carrollton Ave hits the river and you're in the heart of the Riverbend. College kids, local characters and Uptown swells drop into **Cooter Brown's** (☎504-866-9104; www.cooterbrowns.com; 509 S Carrollton Ave; ⊙11am-late; 🐾) for brews and freshly shucked oysters, or to shoot pool or watch sports on TV.

3 Camellia Grill

The **Camellia** (☎504-309-2679; 626 S Carrollton Ave; mains $4-11; ⊙8am-midnight Sun-Thu, to 2am Fri & Sat) is an institution, the place everyone remembers going to for cheap burgers after an evening out. We recommend peoplep at this iconic cornerstone of the 'hood, where the staff call each other – and you – 'baby.'

4 Yvonne La Fleur

They don't make them like this anymore – neither the clothes, millinery or lingerie for sale in **Yvonne La Fleur** (☎504-866-9666; www.yvonnelafleur.com; 8131 Hampson St; ⊙10am-6pm Mon-Sat, to 8pm Thu) nor Yvonne herself, a perfumed businesswoman who has outfitted generations of local ladies for weddings, debuts and race days.

5 Ba Chi Canteen

Don't be skeptical of the bacos at **Ba Chi** (www.facebook.com/bachicanteenla; 7900 Maple St; mains $4-15; ⊙11am-2:30pm Mon-Fri, to 3:30pm Sat, 5:30-9pm Mon-Wed, 5:30-10pm Thu-Sat). These pillowy bundles of deliciousness merge the subtle seasonings of Vietnamese fillings with the foldable convenience of a taco-shaped steamed flour bun. Pho and *banh mi* – dubbed po'boys here – round out the menu.

6 Maple Street Book Shop

This beloved **book shop** (www.maplestreetbookshop.com; 7523 Maple St; ⊙10am-6pm Mon-Sat, 11am-5pm Sun) celebrated its 50th anniversary in 2014. Founded by sisters Mary Kellogg and Rhoda Norman, it is one of the most socially engaged, well-stocked bookshops in the city. Frequent literary events are held throughout the year.

7 Carrollton Ave

The houses that line Carrollton aren't quite as palatial as the mansions on Uptown's pretty St Charles Ave. That's OK; the actual live oaks and leaf cover are as impressive as any other street in New Orleans.

8 Oak Street

Oak St is one of the main drags in the Riverbend. On Tuesday nights in particular folks from across the city flock to the **Maple Leaf Bar** (☎504-866-9359; www.mapleleafbar.com; 8316 Oak St; usually $10, Mon free; ⊙3pm-late) to watch the vaunted Rebirth brass band. But in truth, any night of the week is a good time at this classic venue.

Explore

Mid-City &
Bayou St John

The French Quarter is famous; the Marigny is artsy; the Garden District is fancy. And Mid-City? Mid-City is nice, and we don't mean that in a vanilla way. It's simply pleasant, one of the few neighborhoods remaining in New Orleans that really mixes up income brackets and race. Nearby Bayou St John is the city's own lovely inland waterway.

The Sights in a Day

☀ You'll need a bicycle or car to get around this large neighborhood, as sites can be spread out. Have breakfast and a classy coffee at the **Pagoda Cafe** (p112), then head up beautiful Esplanade Ave all the way to the great, green goodness of **City Park** (p106). Head into the **New Orleans Museum of Art** (p110) and stroll the **Sydney & Walda Besthoff Sculpture Garden** (p110). If the weather's nice, you won't want to leave in a hurry.

☀ Fuel up with a coffee and a beignet at **Morning Call** (p107), then proceed along lovely Bayou St John; the **Pitot House** (p110) is a pleasant spot for learning a little New Orleans history. Get to the other end of the bayou and head for the **Parkway Tavern** (p112). Order a po'boy and bring it to the green banks of the bayou for a picnic lunch.

☾ Now that night is setting, roll on to **Mandina's** (p113) for a classic New Orleans family-style dinner. Afterwards, make for **Twelve Mile Limit** (p113) and enjoy an excellent cocktail.

◉ Top Sights
City Park (p106)

♥ Best of New Orleans

Eating
Parkway Tavern (p112)

Café Degas (p112)

Live Music
Chickie Wah Wah (p114)

Bars & Clubs
Twelve Mile Limit (p113)

Treo (p113)

Museums
New Orleans Museum of Art (p110)

Architecture
Pitot House (p110)

Getting There

🚋 **Streetcar** The City Park spur of Canal St hits Carrollton Ave, then heads up that road all the way to City Park.

🚌 **Bus** No 91 runs up Esplanade Ave, turns into Mid-City and drops by City Park. No 27 follows Louisiana Ave, and also hits the park. The 94 bus runs along Broad, cutting through Mid-City.

🚗 **Car** Free street parking is plentiful.

JOHN COLETTI/GETTY IMAGES ©

Top Sights
City Park

Live oaks, Spanish moss and lazy bayous frame this masterpiece of urban planning. Three miles long and 1 mile wide, dotted with gardens, waterways, bridges and one captivating art museum, City Park is bigger than Central Park in NYC, and it's New Orleans' prettiest green space. It's also a perfect expression of a local 'park,' in the sense that it is an only slightly tamed expression of the Louisiana wetlands – Bayou Metairie runs through the grounds – and hardwood forests.

Map p108, E1

504-482-4888

www.neworleanscitypark.com

Esplanade & City Park Aves

Don't Miss

Peristyle

Looking like a temple to a Greek goddess over-looking Bayou Metairie, the Peristyle is a classical pavilion topped by Ionic columns, built in 1907. Four concrete lions stand watch, while weddings, dances, recitals and curious visitors pass through (and commercials are occasionally shot). A nearby playground is extremely popular with local families.

Storyland

There are no rides at **Storyland** (adult/child $4/free; 🕙10am-5pm Tue-Fri, to 6pm Sat & Sun) but the fairy-tale statuary provides plenty of fuel for young imaginations. Kids can climb Lewis Carroll's Jabberwock, or enter the mouth of the whale from *Pinocchio*. If these characters seem strangely similar to Mardi Gras floats, it's because they were created by master float-builder Blaine Kern.

Botanical Gardens

Local and international flora is exhibited in these **gardens** (🕿504-483-9386; adult/child $4/free; 🕙10am-4:30pm Tue-Sun), where the best display of blooms are in March and April. The fascinating Train Garden replicates the city in 1:22 scale miniature size, cut through with 1300ft of rail.

Carousel Gardens

Charmingly dated **Carousel Gardens** (adult/child $4/free, rides $4; 🕙10am-5pm Tue-Thu, 10am-10pm Fri, 11am-10pm Sat, 11am-6pm Sun Jun & July, Sat & Sun only spring & fall) is a lovingly restored antique carousel housed in a 1906 structure with a stained-glass cupola. In the 1980s, residents raised $1.2 million to restore the animals, fix the merry-go-round and replace the Wurlitzer organ. The results are spectacular, in a tweedy kind of way.

☑ Top Tips

▶ Restrooms are tough to find in City Park. The Morning Call cafe is the best bet.

▶ Parking can become an issue during major events at the park (ie the Voodoo Experience); plan accordingly.

▶ While many let their dogs run off-leash in the park, it's technically a no-no unless you're at City Bark dog park; to get in there, you need a permit, available on the park's website.

✕ Take a Break

Morning Call (www.neworleanscitypark.com; Dreyfous Ave, City Park; $2-10; 🕙24hr) is the natural refueling zone on the grounds of City Park for coffee and beignets.

One of the most romantic dinners in New Orleans is enjoying a fine French meal while the evening sets in at Café Degas (p112).

A
B
C
D

1

Canal Blvd
General Diaz St
Delgado Community College
Orleans Ave
Marconi Dr
Victory Ave

Pontchartrain Blvd

Holt Cemetery

Metairie Cemetery

St Patrick Cemetery

City Park Ave

Helena St
N Anthony St
N Bernadotte St
N St Patrick St
Hennessey St

2

Metairie Rd

Cemeteries

Greenwood & Cypress Grove Cemetery

10

N Olympia St
N Murat St
N Alexander St
Toulouse St
Lafitte Ave
Rosedale Dr

New Orleans Country Club

S Bernadotte St
S Patrick St
S Olympia St
15
Cleveland St
S Murat St
S Alexander St
S Hennessy St
S Solomon St
Canal St
Bienville St

3

Heaton St
Hamilton St
Hollygrove St
Pear St
Marks St

D'Hemecourt St

N Carrollton Ave

9

MID-CITY
Palmyra St

Airline Hwy

Ulloa St

Banks St
Baudin St
14

4

Hollygrove St
General Ogden St
Eagle St
Monroe St
Palmetto St

Dublin St

61

S Pierce St
S Scott St
S Cortez St
12
S Telemachus St
S Genois St
S Clark St
11

S Carrollton Ave

Stroelitz St
Palm St

Xavier University

10

16

Pontchartrain Expwy

For reviews see

◉	Top Sights	p106
◉	Sights	p110
✖	Eating	p112
🍷	Drinking	p113
✿	Entertainment	p114
🔒	Shopping	p115

N
0   1 km
0   0.5 miles

E

City Park

1 New Orleans Museum of Art

2

Sydney & Walda Besthoff Sculpture Garden

LeLong Dr

City Park & Museum of Art

F

Wisner Blvd

Leda St

Moss St

3 Pitot House

Alcee Fortier Park

4

5

7

Maurepas St

Ponce de Leon St

Grande Route St John

G

Belfort Ave

ESPLANADE RIDGE

Fair Grounds Race Track

Fortin St

Esplanade Ave

Desoto St

Le Pagu St

H

Gentilly Blvd

Gayoso St

Dupre St

Paul Murphy St

1

2

David St

Allard Blvd

10

19

18 Orleans Ave

N Carrollton Ave

Delgado Dr

Bayou St John

BAYOU ST JOHN

Orleans Ave

Conti St

N Cortez St

Bienville St

Iberville St

N Jefferson Davis Pkwy

N Hagan Ave

13

N Rendon St

N Lopez St

N Salcedo St

St Peter St

Toulouse St

Lafitte Ave

N Gayoso St

N Dupre St

N White St

6

Bell St

Ursulines Ave

St Philip St

Dumaine St

90

St Ann St

Kerlerec St

8

Barracks St

Governor Nicholls St

Rocheblave St

N Tonti St

N Miro St

N Galvez St

3

4

Jefferson Davis Pkwy

Cleveland Ave

S Jefferson Davis Pkwy

S Rendon St

S Lopez St

S Salcedo St

S Gayoso St

S Dupre St

N Dupre St

N White St

17

White St

Broad St

N Broad Ave

N Dorgenois St

N Rocheblave St

N Tonti St

N Miro St

Orleans Ave

Lafitte St

Toulouse St

St Louis St

5

Tulane Ave

Gravier St

S Broad Ave

61 90

Palmyra St

Canal St

Galvez St

N Galvez St

N Johnson St

N Prieur St

N Roman St

10

Sights

New Orleans Museum of Art

MUSEUM

1 Map p108, E1

Inside City Park, this elegant museum was opened in 1911 and is well worth a visit both for its special exhibitions and top-floor galleries of African, Asian, Native American and Oceanic art – don't miss the outstanding Qing dynasty snuff-bottle collection. Its sculpture garden contains a cutting-edge collection in lush, meticulously planned grounds. (NOMA; ☑504-658-4100; www.noma.org; 1 Collins Diboll Circle; adult/child 7-17yr $10/6; ⊙10am-6pm Tue-Thu, to 9pm Fri, 11am-5pm Sat & Sun)

Understand
Bayou St John

Today, Bayou St John is a pleasant backdrop for a stroll or a short paddle in a kayak. But take a closer look. This sometimes smelly creek is the reason this city exists. It was originally used by Native Americans as a wet highway to the relatively high ground of Esplanade Ridge, but then French explorers realized the waterway was the shortest route between the Mississippi River – and by extent the Gulf of Mexico – and Lake Pontchartrain.

Sydney & Walda Besthoff Sculpture Garden

GARDENS

2 Map p108, E1

Adjacent to NOMA in City Park, this garden opened in 2003 with pieces from the world-renowned Besthoff collection and today holds more than 60 pieces, dotted across 5 acres. Most are contemporary works by such artists as Antoine Bourdelle, Henry Moore and Louise Bourgeois. Admission is free, and it's a pleasant place to stroll. (☑504-488-2631; www.noma.org; 1 Collins Diboll Circle; admission free; ⊙10am-6pm Mon-Fri, to 5pm Sat & Sun)

Pitot House

HISTORIC BUILDING

3 Map p108, F2

The Pitot House, perched prettily beside Bayou St John, is an excellent example of classical French New Orleans architecture. Constructed c 1799, it's the only Creole Colonial house along the bayou that is open to the public. The shaded verandah served as a living area whenever the weather got too hot. The house is named for resident James Pitot, who served as first mayor of incorporated New Orleans and lived here from 1810 to 1819. Visitation is by guided tour. (☑504-482-0312; www.pitot house.org; 1440 Moss St; adult/child under 12yr & senior $7/5; ⊙10am-3pm Wed-Sat)

Alcee Fortier Park

PARK

4 Map p108, G2

This pretty park, strung up with lights and lanterns and decked out

Understand

Hurricane Katrina

New Orleans has long lived in fear of the one powerful storm that could wipe out the city. On the morning of Saturday August 28, 2005, Hurricane Katrina prepared to lay claim to that title.

Mayor Ray Nagin ordered a mandatory evacuation, the first in the city's history. Four out of five residents left, but nearly 200,000 stayed behind, including those who could not find transportation and those who wanted to protect their homes and businesses.

The storm weakened from a Category 5 to a Category 3 before making landfall, but while house-flattening winds are the most celebrated feature of hurricanes, in this case the most deadly aspect was the storm surge, the rising tide of water driven inland by the gales. Katrina's winds pushed water from the Gulf of Mexico up the Mississippi River, into Lake Pontchartrain, and through the canals that lace the city.

The levees did not hold. A torrent of water submerged 80% of the city in a toxic soup of water, gasoline, chemicals, human waste and dead bodies. The massive pumps that clear the city after rainy days couldn't process the volume of water, which rose as high as 15ft in some areas. The 'Sliver by the River' – Uptown, the Garden District, the French Quarter and parts of the Marigny and Bywater – survived unscathed. Elsewhere, people broke into stores, some taking food and medication, others taking luxuries such as DVDs and flat-screen TVs.

Around 26,000 people took shelter at the increasingly squalid Superdome, while others took ad hoc shelter in the Convention Center. Some attempted to walk across a bridge into neighboring Jefferson Parish, only to find their way blocked by police. Officials said evacuees were not allowed out of the city because neighboring areas didn't have sufficient facilities to aid them, but also claimed New Orleanians would bring looting and lawlessness into their communities.

The major takeaway in the wake of the storm, and the mantra repeated by New Orleanians to this day, was that Katrina was not, despite appearances, a natural disaster. Rather, a weather event had come up against poor infrastructure that was desperately in need of updating.

with funky furniture, sits across the road from one of the most attractive stretches of Esplanade, an area replete with restaurants, shops and a general breezy ambience. Movies are sometimes screened here on evenings, especially for kids. (3100 Esplanade Ave)

Eating

Liuzza's by the Track

DINER $

5 Map p108, G2

Mmmm, that gumbo. This quintessential Mid-City neighborhood joint does some of the best in town. The barbecue shrimp po'boy is to die for and the deep-fried garlic oysters are legendary. All that said, the real reason to come is the atmosphere: we've seen a former city judge and a stripper dining together here, which is as 'Only in New Orleans' an experience as you can get. (☑504-218-7888; www.liuzzasnola.com; 1518 N Lopez St; mains $7-16; ☉11am-7pm Mon-Sat)

 Local Life
Angelo Brocato

Opened in 1905, **Angelo Brocato** (☑504-486-1465; www.angelobrocato icecream.com; 214 N Carrollton Ave; scoop of gelato $3.25, pastries under $4; ☉11am-5pm Tue-Sat) is the oldest ice-cream shop in New Orleans. Inside, silky gelatos, perfect cannoli and crispy biscotti catch the eye and wow the taste buds.

Parkway Tavern

SANDWICHES $

6 Map p108, F3

Who makes the best po'boy in New Orleans? Honestly, who can say? But tell a local you think the top sandwich comes from Parkway and you will get, at the least, a nod of respect. The roast beef in particular – a craft some would say is dying among the great po'boy makers – is messy as hell and twice as good. (☑504-482-3047; www.parkwaypoorboys.com; 538 Hagan Ave; po'boys under $13; ☉11am-10pm Wed-Mon)

Café Degas

FRENCH $$

7 Map p108, G2

A pecan tree thrusts through the floor and ceiling of the enclosed deck that serves as Café Degas' congenial dining room. A rustic, romantic little spot, Degas warms the heart with first-rate French fare. Meals that sound familiar on the menu – steak *frites au poivre*, parmesan-crusted veal medallions – are arranged with extraordinary beauty on the plate. (☑504-945-5635; www.cafe degas.com; 3127 Esplanade Ave; mains lunch $11-17, dinner $19-30; ☉11am-3pm & 6-10pm Wed-Sat, 10:30am-3pm & 6-9:30pm Sun)

Pagoda Cafe

CAFE $

8 Map p108, H3

In a land of dimly lit dive bars and heavy Creole buffets, Pagoda Cafe is a sprightly diversion. This compact place serves healthy fare with a global spin. In the morning, look for bacon-and-egg tacos, toast with Nutella and bananas, and housemade granola. For lunch to-go, grab a turnover or a sausage pastry, or settle in for a lemongrass tofu *banh mi*. (www.pagodacafe.net; 1430 N Dorgenois St; breakfast $3-8, pastries under $5, sandwiches $8-10; ⏰7am-4pm Tue-Sat, 9am-3pm Sun; 📶🍴)

Mandina's
ITALIAN $$

9 Map p108, D3

In the Italian American New Orleans community, funerals were followed by a visit to this institution for turtle soup. The menu may be conservative, but when you've been around for more than 100 years you stick to what you know. In this case that's Sicilian Louisiana food: trout almandine, red beans and veal cutlets, and bell peppers stuffed with macaroni and meat. (📞504-482-9179; www.mandinasrestaurant. com; 3800 Canal St; mains $12-20; ⏰11am-9:30pm Mon-Thu, to 10pm Fri & Sat, noon-9pm Sun)

Toup's Meatery
LOUISIANAN $$

10 Map p108, E2

Cheese plates. Charcuterie boards. These are standard appetizers at restaurants across the land. But they are nothing compared to the chest-pounding glory that is the Toup's Meatery Board, a Viking-worthy platter of MEAT. Housemade and cured, this carnivore's feast will harden your arteries in a single glance. But oh, that butter-soft marrow on the bone. (📞504-252-4999; www.toupsmeatery.com; 845 N Carrollton Ave; lunch $15-22, small plates $7-21, dinner $18-29; ⏰11am-2:30pm Tue-Sat, 5-10pm Tue-Thu, 5-11pm Fri & Sat)

Drinking

Twelve Mile Limit
BAR

11 Map p108, D4

Twelve Mile is simply a great bar. It's staffed by people who have the skill, both behind the bar and in the kitchen, to work in four-star spots, but who chose to set up shop in a neighborhood, for a neighborhood. The mixed drinks are excellent, the match of any mixologist's cocktail in Manhattan, and the vibe is super accepting. (500 S Telemachus St; ⏰5pm-midnight Mon-Thu, to 2am Fri & Sat, to 11pm Sun)

Treo
COCKTAIL BAR

12 Map p108, D4

Let's Get Figgy With It. Beetin' Down the Block. Rob Ford. The Homewre... Wait a minute, did Treo just name one of its drinks after Toronto's hard-partying mayor? We like your saucy style, Treo – and your thoughtfully crafted cocktails. This stylish new spot is luring crowds to a re-energized Tulane Ave. Tipplers have a choice of seasonal drinks and Louisiana-style small plates. (☏504-304-4878; www.treonola.com; 3835 Tulane Ave; ⊙11:30am-11pm Tue-Thu, to midnight Fri & Sat)

Pal's
BAR

🔟 13 🍷 Map p108, F3

This great neighborhood bar is a little more convivial for the older generation, although it's definitely an all-ages crowd. The men's bathroom, wallpapered with vintage pinups, is like a walk through *Playboy* history, while the backroom air hockey is always enjoyable. Open until at least 3am Sunday through Thursday, and at least 4am on Friday and Saturday. (www.palslounge.com; 949 N Rendon St; ⊙3pm-late)

Finn McCool's
BAR

14 🍷 Map p108, D4

Want a surreal New Orleans experience? Arrive at 6am when premier league soccer or big international rugby games are playing. You'll see an odd mix of European sports enthusiasts, British expats and local Hispanic packed into this neighborhood bar. Finn's is an excellent spot for a beer any time (especially during St Paddy's Day), but we particularly love it for watching soccer. (☏504-486-9080; www.finnmccools.com; 3701 Banks St; ⊙11am-3am Mon-Fri, 9am-3am Sat, 10am-3am Sun)

Mid-City Yacht Club
BAR

15 🍷 Map p108, C3

The Yacht Club is so much a part of the neighborhood that one of the owners took his boat out to save flooded Katrina victims (hence the name of the bar, which isn't near a lake or ocean). More than this, it is literally a part of the neighborhood: the bar is made from wood salvaged from storm debris. (☏504-483-2517; www.midcityyachtclub.com; 440 S St Patrick St; ⊙11:30am-3pm Mon-Thu, to 3:30am Fri, 10:30am-4am Sat & Sun)

Entertainment

Mid-City Rock & Bowl
LIVE MUSIC

16 ⭐ Map p108, B5

A night at the Rock & Bowl is a quintessential New Orleans experience. The venue is a strange, wonderful combination of bowling alley, deli and huge live-music and dance venue, where patrons get down to New Orleans roots music while trying to avoid that 7-10 split. The best time and place in the city to experience zydeco is the weekly Thursday-night dance party held here. (☏504-861-1700; www.rockandbowl.com; 3000 S Carrollton Ave; ⊙5pm-late)

Chickie Wah Wah
LIVE MUSIC

17 ⭐ Map p108, F4

Despite the fact it lies in Mid-City on one of the most unremarkable

RAY LASKOWITZ/GETTY IMAGES ©

Bayou St John

stretches of Canal St as you please, Chickie Wah Wah is a great jazz club. Local legends such as the Sweet Olive String Band or Meschya Lake, and plenty of international talent, all make their way across the small stage. (☎504-304-4714; www.chickiewahwah.com; 2828 Canal St; ⏰shows around 8pm)

Shopping

Tubby & Coos   BOOKS

18 🔒 Map p108, E2

Haven't found the droids you were looking for? Then stop by this self-proclaimed 'geeky' bookstore where books and movies loved by nerds take the spotlight. *Game of Thrones, Dr Who, Star Wars* – the gang is all here. The slogan for the store's Dungeons & Dating trivia night is boss: 'Eat snacks. Meet nerds. Play trivia.' (☎504 598 5536; www.tubbyandcoos.com; 631 N Carrollton Ave; ⏰10am-7pm Thu-Tue; 🛜)

SoPo   CLOTHING, GIFTS

19 🔒 Map p108, E2

A warm welcome is the first thing you notice at SoPo, which stands for Southern Posh. Boutique women's wear, which is found upstairs, and gifts with Southern flair are the focus. (☎504-609-2429; www.soponola.com; 629 N Carrollton Ave; ⏰10am-6pm Tue-Sat)

Explore

Tremé

The Tremé, one of the oldest African American neighborhoods in the country, is the nexus of a multitude of cultural currents that make New Orleans one of the most distinctive cities in the world. The music, arts and architecture of the African diaspora and Colonial France and Spain come together here like nowhere else in the city.

JOHN COLETTI/GETTY IMAGES ©

The Sights in a Day

☀ The Tremé is a decent-sized neighborhood, so you may want to bicycle as you explore it. Start the day with breakfast at **Lil' Dizzy's** (p123), a cornerstone of the local diner scene. Then walk, or cycle, down Governor Nicholls St and soak up some of the prettiest streetscapes in New Orleans. Make a pit stop at **Le Musée de f.p.c.** (p121), then head to **St Augustine's Church** (p120).

☼ Visit the **Backstreet Cultural Museum** (p120) and leave with a greater appreciation for the unique Caribbean influence that infuses the city. Afterwards, stroll or ride in **Louis Armstrong Park** (p120), or if you're hungry, proceed directly to lunch at **Willie Mae's** (p123) or **Dooky Chase** (p123). Go to the former for transcendent fried chicken, and the latter for some of the best soul food in the country.

☾ As evening sets in, grab some gumbo or a shrimp po'boy (or both) at **Cajun Seafood** (p123). If it's a Wednesday night, you can then move to the **Candlelight Lounge** (p124) for some music. On other nights, **K-Doe's Mother-in-Law Lounge** (p124) is always a great spot for rubbing shoulders with local characters.

 Best of New Orleans

Eating
Willie Mae's Scotch House (p123)

Dooky Chase (p123)

Live Music
Candlelight Lounge (p124)

Museums
Backstreet Cultural Museum (p120)

Parks & Gardens
Louis Armstrong Park (p120)

Getting There

🚌 **Bus** No 91 runs up Esplanade Ave past the Tremé. No 94 runs along Broad St, at the north end of the Tremé.

🚗 **Car** Free street parking is plentiful.

A   B   C   D

1

St Phillip St

Ursulines Ave

N White St

90

◉ 6

N Salcedo St

N Gavoso St

N Dupre St

Esplanade Ave

Le Musée de f.p.c. ◉
5

Barracks St

St Ann St

N White St

Governor Nicholls St

2

St Peter St

Orleans Ave

St Phillip St

Ursulines Ave

Toulouse St

Dumaine St

Rocheblave St

N Tonti St

N Broad Ave

Lafitte St

N Miro St

N Galvez St

N Johnson St

3

N White St

7 ✗

N Prieur St

90

8 ✗

St Ann St

Orleans Ave

N Dorgenois St

N Rocheblave St

N Tonti St

N Miro St

Lafitte Ave

4

⬚ Broad St

Bienville St

Toulouse St

Canal St

Iberville St

St Louis St

N Galvez St

N Johnson St

Conti St

N Prieur St

⬚ Galvez St

N Roman St

N Derbigny St

N Claiborne Ave

10

For reviews see	
◉ Sights	p120
✗ Eating	p123
★ Entertainment	p124

5

Canal St

N
0   500 m
0   0.25 Miles

Sights

Backstreet Cultural Museum

MUSEUM

1 Map p118, G4

Mardi Gras Indian suits grab the spotlight with dazzling flair – and finely crafted detail – in this informative museum, which examines the distinctive elements of African American culture in New Orleans. The museum isn't terribly big – it's the former Blandin's Funeral Home – but if you have any interest in the suits and rituals of Mardi Gras Indians as well as Second Line parades and Social Aid & Pleasure Clubs (the local black community version of civic associations), you need to stop by. (☎504-522-4806; www.backstreetmuseum.org; 1116 Henriette Delille St, formerly St Claude Ave; admission $8; ☉10am-5pm Tue-Sat)

St Augustine's Church

CHURCH

2 Map p118, G4

Open since 1841, 'St Aug's' is the second-oldest African American Catholic church in the country, a place where Creoles, émigrés from St Domingue and free persons of color could worship shoulder to shoulder, even as separate pews were designated for slaves. The future of the church remains in question, so try to visit; more visitors increases the chance of preserving this historic landmark. (☎504-525-5934; www.staugustinecatholicchurch-neworleans. org; 1210 Governor Nicholls St)

Louis Armstrong Park

PARK

3 Map p118, F5

The entrance to this massive park has got to be one of the greatest gateways in the USA, a picturesque arch that

---

Understand
Mardi Gras Indians

The most significant African American tradition of Carnival began in 1885 when a Mardi Gras Indian gang, calling itself the Creole Wild West, paraded the city's backstreets on Mardi Gras. Their elaborately beaded and feathered suits and headdresses made a huge impression, and many more black Indian gangs soon followed – the Wild Tchoupitoulas, Yellow Pocahontas and Golden Eagles, among many others.

The new tradition, some say, signified respect for Native Americans who fought US expansion in the New World. A canon of black Indian songs was passed down from generation to generation, with lyrics often fusing English, Creole French, Choctaw and African words until their meaning was obscure.

Over the years, black Indian suits gained recognition as extravagant works of folk art. Layers of meaningful mosaics are designed and created in patterns of neatly stitched sequins. The making of a new suit can take up to a year.

KYLIE MCLAUGHLIN/GETTY IMAGES ©

Mansions, Esplanade Avenue (p123)

ought rightfully be the final set piece in a period drama about Jazz Age New Orleans. The original Congo Sq (p124) is here, as well as a **Louis Armstrong statue** and a **bust of Sidney Bechet**. The Mahalia Jackson Theater (p124) hosts opera and Broadway productions. (701 N Rampart St; ☺8am-6pm)

New Orleans African American Museum   MUSEUM

4 ◉ Map p118, F3

At press time this small museum was in the midst of a $6 million renovation and closed to visitors. Before closing, the museum displayed an eclectic mix of exhibits mainly dating from slavery and Reconstruction. It's an interesting spot just by dint of its loca-

tion: the Meilleur-Goldthwaite House, also known as the Tremé Villa. This pretty house was the site of the city's first brick yard and is an exemplar of the Creole architectural style. In the back are restored shotgun houses and slave quarters. (☎504-566-1136; www. noaam.org; 1418 Governor Nicholls St; adult/student/child $7/5/3; ☺11am-4pm Wed-Sat)

Le Musée de f.p.c.   MUSEUM

5 ◉ Map p118, D1

Inside a lovely 1859 Greek-revival mansion in the Upper Tremé, this museum showcases a 30-year collection of artifacts, documents, furniture and art. It all tells the story of a forgotten subculture: the 'free people of color' before the Civil War, who played a

Understand

The Backstreet

New Orleans is popularly known as the most European city in the USA; however, in an immediate and visceral way it is more Caribbean. Local African American culture is a unique product of myriad folkways, many of which can be traced to the Caribbean Islands from where slaves were imported, and so by extension to West Africa.

Cultural practices survived and thrived among the enslaved and free ancestors of black New Orleanians. This was due to French slavery laws, which allowed for (relatively) more freedom of expression and celebration of ancestral roots than the American slavery system.

Collectively, these influences are known as the Backstreet, a name that alludes to the way this face of New Orleans culture is, like the African American communities where it manifests, an entity both part of and separate from the mainstream experience of New Orleans.

The Tremé is in the heart of the New Orleans Backstreet, and the easiest way of accessing this culture is a visit to the Backstreet Cultural Museum (p120). Here is some background on two important elements of the Backstreet.

Voodoo

Voodoo, far from its clichéd spells and sorcery stereotype, is a living, functioning faith practiced throughout New Orleans, although the exact number of followers hasn't been determined. Originating in West Africa, it is a belief system that stresses ancestor worship and the presence of the divine via a pantheon of spirits and deities. Slaves from Africa and the Caribbean brought voodoo to Louisiana, where it melded with Roman Catholicism.

Second Lines

Second Lines are neighborhood parades that proceed through the city's African American neighborhoods. They occur every Sunday from roughly September to June, and are a fascinating insight into local life. Visitors are always welcome, but be prepared for a scene that includes a lot of loud music, public drinking and unabashed public dancing. Check out the 'Takin' It to the Streets' section of WWOZ.org for information on when (and if) a Second Line is occurring during your visit.

unique but prominent role in the development of the city. The small but fascinating collection includes original documentation of slaves who became free, either by *coartación* (buying their own freedom) or as a reward for particularly good service. (Free People of Color Museum; 504-914-5401; www.lemuseedefpc.com; 2336 Esplanade Ave; tour adult/student & senior $15/10; noon-4:40pm Sat & Sun)

Esplanade Avenue STREET

6 Map p118, C1

Esplanade is one of the most beautiful streets in New Orleans, yet barely recognized by visitors as such. Because of the abundance of historical homes, Esplanade, which follows the 'high ground' of Esplanade Ridge, is known as the Creole St Charles Ave. Both streets are shaded by rows and rows of leafy live oaks, but whereas St Charles is full of large, plantation-style American villas, Esplanade is framed by columned, French Creole–style mansions. (btwn Rampart St & City Park)

Eating

Willie Mae's Scotch House SOUTHERN $

7 Map p118, C3

Willie Mae's has been dubbed some of the best fried chicken in the world by the James Beard Foundation, the Food Network and other media. It thus sees a steady flow of tourist traffic. The chicken, served in a basket, is pretty damn good, as are the butter beans. (2401 St Ann St; fried chicken $11; 10am-5pm Mon-Sat)

Dooky Chase SOUTHERN, CREOLE $$

8 Map p118, C3

Ray Charles wrote 'Early in the Morning' about Dooky's; civil rights leaders used it as informal headquarters in the 1960s, and Barack Obama ate here after his inauguration. Leah Chase's labor of love is the backbone of the Tremé, and her buffets are the stuff of legend. Top-notch gumbo and excellent fried chicken are served in a white-linen dining room to office workers and ladies who lunch. (504-821-0600; 2301 Orleans Ave; buffet $20, mains $16-25; 11am-3pm Tue-Thu, 11am-3pm & 5-9pm Fri)

Cajun Seafood SEAFOOD $

9 Map p118, F2

The name says it all: this is a grocery store and takeout that's one of the best budget options in town for raw seafood and cooked hot plates, such as fried chicken, boudin, fish plates and the like. The boiled shrimp are always freakishly huge, as are the shrimp po'boys. (504-948-6000; 1479 N Claiborne Ave; takeout $5-19; 10:30am-9pm)

Lil' Dizzy's LOUISIANAN, CREOLE $

10 Map p118, F3

One of the city's great lunch spots, Dizzy's does mean soul food specials in a historic shack owned by the Baquet family, who have forever been part of the culinary backbone of New Orleans. The fried chicken is excellent, the hot sausages may be better and the bread pudding is divine. (📞504-569-8997; www.lildizzyscafe.com; 1500 Esplanade Ave; breakfast $7-14, lunch $10-16, buffet $16-18; ⏰7am-2pm Mon-Sat, 8am-2pm Sun)

Entertainment

Candlelight Lounge LIVE MUSIC

 Map p118, E4

Deep in the Tremé, the Candlelight looks like a bunker on the outside and...a slightly nicer bunker on the inside. Most nights it's a neighborhood bar, but on Wednesdays around 10pm (and occasionally other nights) it hosts the Tremé Brass Band ($10 cover), one of the most enjoyable live sets in the city. This is as wonderful as local music gets in this town. (📞504-525-4728; 925 N Robertson St; ⏰2pm-late)

Mahalia Jackson Theater THEATER

 Map p118, F4

Hosts performances of the **New Orleans Ballet Association** (www. nobadance.com) and productions from the **New Orleans Opera** (www.new orleansopera.org) and Broadway. (📞504-525-1052, box office 504-287-0350; www. mahaliajacksontheater.com; 1419 Basin St)

K-Doe's Mother-in-Law Lounge LOUNGE

 Map p118, F2

Ernie K-Doe was famous for writing the song 'Mother-in-Law' and

---

Understand
Congo Square

Within Louis Armstrong Park (p120) is one of the most important spots in the development of modern music: Congo Sq. Under French Colonial law, slaves were allowed to gather here on Sundays. The period of rest became one of both celebration and preservation of West African rituals; it must have been, at the time, the largest celebration of traditional African culture in continental North America – slaves were forbidden from practicing traditional culture in the American colonies.

The practice was shut down when US settlers took over New Orleans, but it was alive long enough to imprint its musical stamp on the city's cultural substrate. By the late 19th century, brass bands were blending African rhythms with classical music, and their sound eventually evolved into jazz – itself a foundation for the variations of pop music (R & B, rock and roll, even hip-hop) the USA would give the world in the 20th century.

LAURI PATTERSON/GETTY IMAGES ©

Cajun shrimp and sausage gumbo

frequently proclaiming his 'Emperorship of the Universe.' His bar, the Mother-in-Law Lounge, was filled with crazy art and homages to the emperor and his empress (dearly departed wife, Antoinette). Now owned by trumpeter Kermit Ruffins, this remains one of the oddest bars in the city. (☏504-947-1078; 1500 N Claiborne Ave; ◷5pm-late)

Saenger Theatre

THEATER

 Map p118, F5

The Saenger's ornate 1927 facade was designed by noted New Orleans architect Emile Weil. It has been refurbished and renovated into one of the finest indoor venues in the city. (☏504-525-1052; www.saengernola.com; 143 N Rampart St)

The Best of
New Orleans

New Orleans' Best Walks

Balconies & Courtyards 128
Garden District Stroll. 130

New Orleans' Best...

Eating 132
Live Music. 134
Shopping 136
Bars & Clubs. 137
Gay & Lesbian 138
For Kids 139
Architecture 140
Tours 142
Festivals 143
Parks & Gardens 144
Museums 145
Theater. 146

Celebrations in Congo Square (p124), Louis Armstrong Park
KRIS DAVIDSON/LONELY PLANET ©

Best Walks
Balconies & Courtyards

🏃 The Walk

The Creole architecture of the French Quarter and proximate neighborhoods represents an aesthetic that is both unique in the USA and typical of Caribbean stylistic elements found across many colonial ports around the world. On this walking tour, be on the lookout for iron balconies that consciously blur the line between public and private space. Behind many of the larger houses you will pass are lush courtyards, a feature imported by the Spanish, who in turn received the tradition from Moorish occupiers in the medieval age.

Start Cake Café & Bakery

Finish Gallier House Museum

Length 0.7 miles; 1½ hours

✕ Take a Break

Verti Marte (p38) is a grungy little take-out stand and a quintessential spot for a po'boy. Order the 'All That Jazz' and thank us after.

RAY LASKOWITZ/GETTY IMAGES ©

Classic French Quarter architecture

❶ Chartres St

Start the walk in the Marigny with a bite at the **Cake Café & Bakery** (p51). When you're done, head 'up,' which is to say 'upriver' (west), on Chartres St and cast your eyes on surrounding blocks, which are largely built up of Creole cottages and shotgun houses, and other forms of living residential historical architecture.

❷ Chartres & Elysian Fields

At **2215 Chartres St** you'll see a single-shotgun home (a row of rooms lacking a connecting corridor); **2211/3 Chartres** is a double shotgun (two adjacent shotgun singles combined into one house). At **2209 Chartres** is a Creole cottage, essentially, a square home subdivided into four squares on the interior with a steeply gabled roof. All of these places are private residences.

❸ Lower Quarter

Continue along Chartres St into the French Quarter. You'll find good examples of iconic multistory French Quarter town houses at **1321**, **1231** and **1229 Chartres** (all private buildings). Look for wrought-iron balconies that run from simple to ornate.

❹ Beauregard-Keyes House

Most of the best courtyards within the Quarter are hidden from tourists. The gardens of 1826 Greek-revival **Beauregard-Keyes House** (p34) can be seen partially from the street, hidden behind hedges. You'll need to pay the entrance fee

to access them. That's OK; the house has a gorgeous interior and is worth your time.

❺ Ursuline Convent

Built in 1752 the **Ursuline Convent** (p34) is the oldest building in the Mississippi River Valley and the oldest surviving example of French Colonial architecture in the country. The imposing stone edifice feels distinctly European; it lacks the Caribbean color and ventilation of other Quarter buildings. There's a serene court-

yard behind the main building.

❻ Gallier House Museum

Many New Orleans buildings owe their existence, either directly or by design, to James Gallier Sr and Jr, who added Greek-revivalist, British and American accents to the Quarter's French/Spanish/Creole architecture mélange. In 1857 Gallier Jr began work on this **town house** (p33), which incorporated all of the above elements.

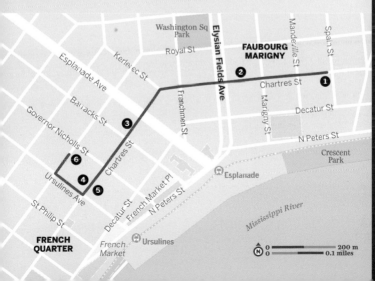

Best Walks
Garden District Stroll

🏃 The Walk

Following the Louisiana Purchase in 1803, Americans began moving to New Orleans. Shunned by the Creole inhabitants, they settled on the other side of Canal St, building plantations upriver from the French Quarter. These upriver communities were essentially suburbs, but trade led to wealth and expansion. Land was parceled out of plantations; these 'garden'-sized lots formed the Garden District. In a display of one-upmanship aimed at the Creoles, as well as a homage to the founders of democracy, many built homes in Greek-revival style – fronted by columns and accented by colonnaded galleries.

Start Goodrich-Stanley House

Finish Walter Grinnan Robinson House

Length 1 mile; 2½ hours

✕ Take a Break

The Avenue Pub (p84) is great for a beer, and for a meal out of its innovative kitchen.

ROBERT HOLMES/CORBIS ©

House of Broel

❶ Goodrich-Stanley House

At 1729 Coliseum St, this historic double-gallery home was built in 1837 by the jeweler William M Goodrich. Goodrich sold the house to the British-born merchant Henry Hope Stanley, whose adopted son, Henry Morton Stanley, went on to gain fame for finding the missing Scottish missionary Dr David Livingstone and uttering the legendary question, 'Dr Livingstone, I presume?'

❷ Grace King House

At 1749 Coliseum St, behind a handsome wrought-iron fence, this papaya-hued house was named for the Louisiana historian and author who lived here from 1905 to 1932. It was built in 1847 by banker Frederick Rodewald, and features Greek Ionic columns on the lower floor as well as Corinthian columns above. Not open to the public.

❸ House of Broel

The **House of Broel** (p83), built in the 1850s, is a bit madcap. The entire two-story building was elevated in 1884 to allow for the construction of a new 1st floor; the owner wanted to throw elaborate parties for his three daughters. Today the house showcases gowns and an astounding collection of highly detailed dollhouses.

❹ McGehee School for Girls

At 2343 Prytania St, the McGehee School for Girls, formerly the **Bradish Johnson House**, looks like a stately opera house

that was dropped in the heart of the Garden District. The 1872 building was designed by James Freret in the Second Empire style, an architectural school not known for its subtlety.

❺ Brevard House

If the home at 1239 First St looks like it could house an aristocratic vampire or a cabal of Southern witches, you've either got a great imagination or have read Anne Rice; this home, known as the **Brevard House**, used to be the author's

residence. The 1857 Greek-revival masterpiece has two stories of columns and wrought-iron balconies.

❻ Walter Grinnan Robinson House

This columned double-decker house sticks out on a relatively modest block of Third St like an exceptionally ornate sore thumb. It was built in 1859 and designed by the famed Irish New Orleans architect Henry Howard. The massive home mixes the grandiosity of both the Greek-revival and Italianate schools.

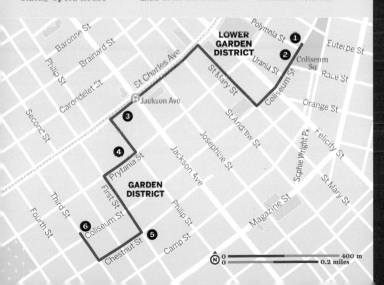

Best Eating

In what other American city do people celebrate the harvest season of sewage-dwelling crustaceans? We're describing a crawfish boil, by the way, which exemplifies New Orleans' relationship with food: unconditional love, particularly of local ingredients. This city finds itself in its food; meals are expressions of identity and bridges between the city's divisions.

Born on the Bayou

Settlers who arrived in Louisiana had to work with the ingredients of the bayous, woods and prairie, and developed one of America's only true native-born cuisines. As a result, some say the New Orleans palette is limited to its own specialties, that this is a town of 'a thousand restaurants and three dishes.' That cliché is a bit tired. First, lots of restaurants are serving what we would deem 'Nouveau' New Orleans cuisine – native classics influenced by global flavors and techniques. Second: international options expand every month.

The Native Nola Menu

It's true that this is a place where homegrown recipes are the best dishes on the menu, and these are staggering in their diversity. Favorites include gumbo, the one-pot wonder; rice-based jambalaya; smoked tasso ham; and rich étouffée, a saucy shellfish concoction poured over rice.

International Influences

New Orleans cuisine isn't just French food plopped in the swamp. Sicilian immigrants fashioned the manhole-sized *muffuletta* sandwich; the Vietnamese created a regional appetite for pho; waves of Hondurans enjoy corn-husk wrapped tamales; and Germans brought an unapologetic love of sausages.

IAIN BAGWELL/GETTY IMAGES ©

Best Breakfast

Surrey's Juice Bar
Divine juice and amazing breakfasts at this artsy, student standby. (p81)

Cake Café & Bakery
Long lines belie the amazing food in this Marigny hot spot. (p51)

Best Vegetarian

Pizza Delicious The cheese pizza is delicious, and there's always a vegan-friendly pie on the menu. (p50)

Green Goddess Eclectic menus and a sense of fun infuse this French Quarter spot. (p39)

Best Po'boys

Mahony's Po-Boy Shop
Offers both creative and classical takes on the iconic sandwich. (p96)

Above left: seafood po-boy; above right: Cajun jambalaya

Domilise's Po-Boys An old shack dripping with character and the scent of fried seafood. (p98)

Guy's Old-school neighborhood spot where every sandwich is carefully made to order. (p98)

Parkway Tavern Much-vaunted neighborhood institution for a classically executed sandwich. (p112)

Best Classic Creole Cuisine

Dooky Chase In the Tremé you'll find the grande dame of African American Creole cookery. (p123)

Gautreau's Haute Southern cuisine, fresh and excellent ingredients, all served in an intimate atmosphere. (p96)

Clancy's A neighborhood Uptown institution for some of New Orleans' most hallowed dishes. (p96)

Restaurant August The most upscale ambassador of the John Besh culinary empire; elegant and delicious. (p67)

Best Romantic Restaurants

Café Degas Classic French fare served in a courtyard with a shade tree. (p112)

Bacchanal Wine and cheese served under the stars, scented with live music. (p50)

Bayona Local ingredients and international influences play out in this excellent French Quarter splurge. (p36)

 Worth a Trip

Head south of New Orleans to the Westbank and the inconspicuous **Tan Dinh** (504-361-8008; 1705 Lafayette St, Gretna; mains $8-17; 9:30am-9pm Mon, Wed-Fri, 9am-9pm Sat, to 8pm Sun), a popular eating spot of Vietnamese immigrants and their children. The prices are good value and the flavors consistently outstanding; the garlic-butter chicken wings and Korean short-ribs are must-tries.

Best
Live Music

New Orleans without music is Washington without politics, or Paris without fashion. In this city of appetites, music feeds the soul. The city's history can be traced in its music, with each genre speaking to ethnic groups, civil rights and cultural influence. Beyond that, social life in New Orleans often revolves around catching a great show.

Mixing Makes Music

Ethnic immersion gave New Orleans its distinctive sounds. The French and their Creole descendants gave the city two opera companies before any other US city had one. Meanwhile, slaves and free persons of color preserved African music in Congo Sq (p124). These influences inexorably came together when French-speaking black Creoles livened up European dance tunes by adding African rhythms. From there, jazz was an inevitability.

Shake Ya Brass

What makes brass music distinct from jazz? It's less improvisational and far more danceable. While some brass bands play traditional music inspired by marching band arrangements of the 19th century, others, such as streetwise Rebirth, fuse styles from 'trad' jazz to funk, hip-hop and R & B.

Discovering Zydeco

It's hard not to move when you hear the raw rhythms of zydeco, the music of the Cajun prairie. Bands almost always comprise a fiddle, accordion, guitar and triangle; the rhythm section usually includes a *frottoir*, a metal washboard that's worn like armor and played with spoons. The Thursday-night zydeco party at Mid-City Rock & Bowl is not to be missed.

KRIS DAVIDSON/LONELY PLANET ©

☑ Top Tips

▶ The best radio stations in New Orleans are WTUL 91.5 FM, and WWOZ 90.7 FM. The former is Tulane University's radio station, which plays an eclectic mix of generally high-quality tunes. The latter, known as 'O-Z,' plays local New Orleans sounds and is a backbone of the city's musical community.

Above left: Snug Harbor; above right: Second Line (p122) jazz parade

Best Brass Bands

d.b.a. A good beer selection and big-name bands. (p53)

Freret Street Publiq House Get funky with local acts on Freret St. (p99)

Tipitina's One of the most iconic names in New Orleans venues. (p100)

Hi Ho Lounge Takes a chance on showcasing younger brass talent. (p54)

Candlelight Lounge The home base of the wonderful Tremé Brass Band. (p124)

Best Jazz

Spotted Cat The epitome of a whiskey-drenched jazz dive. (p54)

Snug Harbor Classy establishment for jazz and a hot date. (p54)

Chickie Wah Wah Eclectic lineups at this Mid-City Institution. (p114)

Preservation Hall The quintessential spot for classic New Orleans jazz. (p42)

Old US Mint Fantastic, free shows pop off at this museum. (p32)

Best Zydeco

Mid-City Rock & Bowl Bowling and zydeco dancing – hard to go wrong. (p114)

Tipitina's Hosts a weekly Cajun dance party. (p100)

House of Blues Acts from all around Louisiana on a regular basis. (p42)

Best
Shopping

Too many travelers assume shopping in New Orleans equals unspeakable T-shirts from the French Quarter. Wrong! New Orleans is a creative town that attracts innovative entrepreneurs and, as such, features all sorts of lovely vintage antiques, cutting-edge boutiques, functional art and amusing kitsch.

LONELY PLANET/GETTY IMAGES ©

Collecting Kitsch

Of course there are some really great awful souvenirs to collect out there: T-shirts, foodstuffs (you're in hot-sauce heaven), Mardi Gras masks, stripper outfits etc... And besides the unintentional kitsch there is quite a bit of intentional tackiness – this city knows how to mock itself.

Art Attack

Music makes New Orleans go round, and this is a fantastic town for buying vinyl and high-quality instruments. A large literary scene has resulted in a good number of independent bookshops, too, some of which have evolved into unofficial anchors of their respective communities.

Best Quirky Gifts

Frenchmen Art Market Find the perfect handcrafted gift at this indie arts market. (p50)

Fifi Mahony's There are wigs and then there are transformative headpieces. Fifi's sells the latter. (p43)

I.J. Reilly's Artsy gifts and knickknacks for the discerning souvenir shopper. (p54)

Best Books & Music

Tubby & Coos A sci-fi-, horror- and fantasy-themed bookstore? Oh yes. (p115)

Crescent City Comics Get lost in this excellent repository of graphic novels and comics. (p101)

Louisiana Music Factory Learn the local music of the state of LA. (p55)

Euclid Records Atmospheric record store for the obsessive music-lover in all of us. (p55)

Best Clothes & Costumes

Funky Monkey Vintage goods and crazy clothes abound at this little shop. (p84)

Uptown Costume & Dancewear Want to dress like a space-age Robin Hood? Then this is where you go. (p101)

SoPo Awesome designs showcasing the best of Southern culture and creativity. (p115)

Best
Bars & Clubs

The stool in an average New Orleans bar has more character than a dozen slick yuppie joints or bog-standard keg shacks. Even the city's craft cocktail spots and sports bars manage to feel idiosyncratic.

How Much?

You'll rarely pay more than $5 for a beer. Sometimes domestics will go for under $3. Cocktails rarely top $6; shots of hard spirits go for around $3 to $5; and everything is cheaper during happy hour. Wine can be pricey at wine bars, but is generally of very high quality.

Bars, Clubs & Lounges

Bars in New Orleans would often be considered 'dives' elsewhere. That's not to say bars here are grotty (although some are); rather, there are many neighborhood joints that cater to drinks as opposed to singles. If you're in the latter category, head to lounges. That said, some bars, such as Mimi's in the Marigny, are good spots for both a beer after work and a bit of random flirtation.

Best Bar Food

Sylvain This gastro pub's menu was created to complement drinks. (p38)

Lost Love Dive bars plus Vietnamese menu equals a lot of boozy grub love. (p52)

Mimi's in the Marigny Small plates of truly innovative bar-based gastronomy. (p52)

KRIS DAVIDSON / LONELY PLANET ©

d.b.a. It's hard to listen to the band when there's this much beer to choose from. (p53)

NOLA Brewing The city's homegrown, fantastically eclectic brewery. (p84)

Best Cocktails

Tonique Cocktails at this bar are taken to a new level of awesome. (p39)

French 75 Classic French Quarter establishment – order the namesake drink! (p40)

Cure The cocktail bar that changed the face of Freret St. (p99)

Twelve Mile Limit Low-key neighborhood bar. (p113)

Treo Nothing complements the on-site art gallery like a fine mixed drink. (p113)

Twelve Mile Limit Nothing chases a beer like tasty barbecue. (p113)

Best Beer

Avenue Pub Enormous beer menu? Check. Great kitchen? Check. (p84)

Freret Street Publiq House This Freret St favorite has a great variety of brews. (p99)

Best
Gay & Lesbian

KYLIE MCLAUGHLIN/GETTY IMAGES ©

Louisiana is a culturally conservative state, but its largest city bucks that trend. New Orleans is one of the oldest gay-friendly cities in the western hemisphere and markets itself as the 'Gay Capitol of the South.' Neighborhoods such as the French Quarter and the Marigny are major destinations on the GLBT travel circuit.

A Long GLBT Legacy

New Orleans has long had a reputation for tolerance. Even today gay and lesbian youth from conservative states such as Alabama and Mississippi feel the pull of the Big Easy, where acceptance of their sexuality is easy to find. Artists such as Tennessee Williams, Truman Capote and Lyle Saxon, among many others, found acceptance and purpose here; Williams went so far as to dub New Orleans his 'spiritual home.' Gay civil rights battles were fought in New Orleans by groups such as the Gertrude Stein Society.

Best Gay-Specific

Faubourg Marigny Book Store Come patronize the oldest gay bookstore in the American South. (p55)

Bourbon Pub & Parade Cheesy dance moves mix with sweaty good times at this club. (p42)

Oz Home to a pumping dance floor, popular with all ages. (p42)

Country Club An outdoor pool, sauna and fantastic bar adds up to a lovely evening. (p52)

Best Gay-Friendly

Fifi Mahony's This wig shop is also an outpost for the queer and trans community. (p43)

Frenchmen Street This local live-music strip is popular with all sexualities. (p49)

Twelve Mile Limit The staff and clientele here make for a decidedly welcoming neighborhood bar. (p113)

Bacchanal A friendly wine and cheese shop that's a popular hangout for big dinner parties. (p50)

Best For Kids

New Orleans is a fairy-tale city, with its colorful beads, weekly costume parties and daily music wafting through the air. The same flights of fancy and whimsy that give this city such appeal for poets and artists also make it an imaginative wonderland for children, especially creative ones.

JUDY BELLAH/GETTY IMAGES ©

Best Parks & Playgrounds

Jackson Square Beignets, sunny days, artwork and soft grass. (p28)

City Park Playgrounds, nature trails and shady live oaks. (p106)

Alcee Fortier Park This bucolic garden hosts regular family-friendly events. (p110)

Crescent Park Pet-friendly park with room for kids to run along the river. (p49)

Audubon Park Huge grassy greens and enormous trees make for a natural wonderland. (p92)

Best Outdoor Adventures

Audubon Zoo This zoo makes a point of holding family-friendly days. (p90)

Storyland Fairy-tale characters emerge from the grounds of City Park. (p107)

Lafayette Cemetery No 1 The inherent creepiness will get young imaginations cranking. (p74)

Best for a Rainy Day

National WWII Museum Older children will appreciate the plethora of interactive displays. (p58)

Aquarium of the Americas Penguins, parakeets and a rare white alligator. (p68)

☑ Top Tips

▶ **Packing** From April until October, New Orleans can be oppressively hot and humid. Pack cool, airy clothes for your kids.

▶ **Strollers** New Orleans' badly maintained sidewalks are often horrible for strollers – you'll want to bring one that is maneuverable and durable.

▶ **High chairs** Most restaurants have high chairs and booster seats and are happy to accommodate kids. Call ahead to make sure, as some places with liquor licenses cannot host patrons under 21.

Best
Architecture

New Orleans has the most distinctive cityscape in the USA. Its character is directly attributable to its quantity of historic homes. The French Quarter and Garden District have long been considered exemplars of New Orleans architecture, but send the Tremé, Marigny or Irish Channel to another city, and they too would stand out as treasure troves of history and heritage.

Skin of the City

There are currently 158 sites in Orleans Parish that are listed on the National Register of Historic Places. While we stress that there's more to the city's architecture than the French Quarter and Garden District, and that many styles of buildings have 'crossed' the lines, as it were, those neighborhoods do illustrate the pronounced difference between the two 'sectors' of New Orleans: Creole and American.

Creole Faubourgs

The French Quarter and the Creole 'faubourgs' (Marigny, Bywater and the Tremé) downriver from Canal St are densely packed with stuccoed brick structures built in various architectural styles and housing types rarely found in other US cities. These areas are where you'll find a glut of candy-colored Euro-Caribbean buildings that seem decidedly transplanted into North America.

Uptown Elegance

Across Canal St from the French Quarter you'll find the wide lots and luxurious houses of the Garden District more closely resemble upscale homes found throughout the South. As you head upriver into the heart of the Garden District and Uptown, the displays of wealth intensify to the point of near-gaudiness.

MEDIOIMAGES/PHOTODISC/GETTY IMAGES ©

☑ **Top Tips**

▶ Have you fallen in love with New Orleans' architecture? Maybe you should take home a piece of it. The **Green Project** (☎504-945-0240; 2831 Marais St; ⊙9am-5pm Mon-Sat) sells reusable building materials culled from local abandoned properties and junked homes. Shop here to spruce up your own place and save a bit of the city's historical heritage.

Above left: New Orleans architecture; above right: ornate balcony, French Quarter

Best 19th-Century & Modern Architecture

New Orleans Museum of Art This imposing edifice is a neoclassical work of art itself. (p110)

Marigny Opera House This theater company is located in the old Holy Trinity Catholic Church. (p53)

Esplanade Avenue Brilliant examples of double-gallery homes and Creole mansions. (p123)

National WWII Museum Soaring ceilings and glass atriums at this modern masterpiece. (p58)

Ogden Museum of Southern Art The main hall is a wonderful exercise in light and space. (p60)

McKenna Museum of African American Art Occupies a lovely two-story historical property not far off St Charles Ave. (p80)

Best Colonial Architecture

Ursuline Convent The grande dame of local French Colonial buildings. (p34)

Cabildo This former seat of government was built by the Spanish. (p26)

Gallier House Museum Historical home combining many elements of New Orleans' architectural heritage. (p33)

Royal Street Packed with Creole town houses that are framed by iron balconies fronting lush courtyards. (p24)

Jackson Square Bracketed on three sides by some of the best architectural gems in town. (p28)

Irish Channel Explore residential historical homes in a sea of shotgun houses. (p80)

Preservation Resource Center Provides in valuable insight into the building heritage of New Orleans. (p66)

Pitot House This Bayou St John home is a classic example of a Creole mansion. (p110)

Old US Mint The oldest extant building to have served as a US Mint. (p32)

St Louis Cathedral One of the finest French Colonial cathedrals in the USA. (p29)

Best
Tours

New Orleans can be an easy city to discover, but it can also hold its secrets close to its chest. A smart and funny tour guide can be the difference between a good trip and a great trip.

KYLIE MCLAUGHLIN/GETTY IMAGES ©

Friends of the Cabildo (📞504-523-3939; www. friendsofthecabildo.org; 523 St Ann St; adult/student $20/15; 🕙10am & 1:30pm Tue-Sun) These excellent walking tours are led by knowledgeable (and often funny) docents who will give you a great primer on the history of the French Quarter, the stories behind some of the most famous streets and details of the area's many architectural styles.

Soul of Nola (📞504-905-4999; www.soulofnola. com; per hr from $100) Tour guide Cassandra Snyder grew up a nomad, fell in love with New Orleans and now leads highly personalized tours of the culture and hidden spaces of New Orleans. If you're looking to get

under the city's skin and want an individualized experience, this is the tour for you. Spanish-language tours available.

Confederacy of Cruisers (📞504-400-5468; www.confederacyofcruisers. com; tours from $49) Get yourself out of the Quarter and on two wheels – this superinformative, laid-back bike tour takes you through Nola's non-Disneyland neighborhoods – Faubourg Marigny, Esplanade Ridge, the Tremé – often with a bar stop along the way.

Tours by Judy (📞504-416-6666; www.toursbyjudy. com; tours from $15) Judy Bajoie, a local scholar and historian, leads well-crafted tours of the city she loves.

New Orleans Culinary History Tours (📞877-278-8240; www.noculinary tours.com; tours from $46) It's hard to beat a tour that is delicious and intellectually stimulating. That's what Kelly Hamilton, a history instructor at Xavier University, offers with tours that plumb both the past and local pantries.

American Photo Safari (📞504-298-8876; www. americanphotosafari.com; Jackson Sq, by St Louis Cathedral; tours from $69) A cleverly focused tour: the photo safari docents don't just show you the sights, they give you lessons in how to take pictures of them as well.

Best
Festivals

RAY LASKOWITZ/GETTY IMAGES ©

New Orleans is a city of festivals. Its celebrations are a function of community expression and a maintenance of rituals that date as far back as Catholic France and pre-Colonial Africa. So when you see folks here partying their butts off, remember that debauchery is, in some ways, a veneration of traditions that have persisted for hundreds of years.

Mardi Gras (www.mardi grasneworleans.com) In February or early March, Fat Tuesday marks the orgasmic finale of the Carnival season.

Jazz Fest (www.nojazzfest. com; ☺Apr-May) The last weekend of April and the first weekend of May; a world-renowned extravaganza of music, food, crafts and good living.

French Quarter Festival (www.fqfi.org) The second weekend of April; multiple stages host the largest free music festival in the country.

Gay Pride New Orleans (www.gayprideneworleans. com) The Gay Pride New Orleans festival, held in June, is embraced by the entire city – a scene that may surprise those used to the generally conservative South.

New Orleans Arts District Arts Walk (www. neworleansartsdistrict.com; Julia St; ☺1st Sat of month) The fine-art galleries in New Orleans Arts District celebrate the opening night of month-long feature-artist exhibitions on the first Saturday of each month from 6pm until close (which is whenever, really).

St Joseph's Day – Super Sunday (☺Mar) March 19 and its nearest Sunday bring 'gangs' of Mardi Gras Indians out into the streets in all their feathered, drumming glory. The Super Sunday parade usually begins around noon at Bayou St John and Orleans Ave, but follows no fixed route.

St Patrick's Day (www. stpatricksdayneworleans. com, ☺Mar) March 17 and its closest weekend see parades of cabbage-wielding Irishfolk.

Tennessee Williams Literary Festival (www. tennesseewilliams.net) Five days of literary panels, plays and parties to celebrate the author's work. Held in March.

Best
Parks & Gardens

New Orleans is a particularly fecund city; roots burst through sidewalks, trees tower over the streets, and you generally get the feeling that if you dropped an apple core, an orchard would grow in its place. It naturally follows that this town has a surfeit of parks that attempt to shape this boundless organic energy.

ANDRE KNUDSEN/GETTY IMAGES ©

A Green Kingdom

Even the landscaped parts of this city have a sense of the primeval, of being wild and woolly. It is the birthright of New Orleans children to grow up against an incredibly green backdrop, where they learn from an early age to avoid clumps of Spanish moss and dirt mounds for fear of fire ants. Yet they also learn to feel no fear when they spot an alligator in a City Park waterway. This is an alive place, and nature is constantly harnessed into something beautiful.

City Park It's hard not to love the largest park in the city. (p106)

Audubon Park Musty, lush live oaks, drapes of Spanish moss and sunning students. (p92)

Crescent Park Great river views and green-laced waterfront paths wind through this popular park. (p49)

Alcee Fortier Park A small lot that's been turned into a wonderland garden. (p110)

Sydney & Walda Besthoff Sculpture Garden Enjoy the outdoors surrounded by some of the region's best sculpture. (p110)

Botanical Gardens A gorgeous collection of plants set in a lovely function area. (p107)

Audubon Zoo Seek out the fascinating exhibits at this spot on a nice-weather day. (p90)

Louis Armstrong Park Big music festivals often kick off in this venue. (p120)

Best
Museums

New Orleans is known for its hedonistic tendencies far more than its cerebral side, but this cliché dismisses an intelligent brain that wants to thoughtfully process the sensory and emotional overload dished out. The city's museums and galleries – a core of well-kept facilities that would easily be the envy of city's of similar size – curate this sensory feast by offering interpretations and context for the aesthetics on display.

IMAGE COURTESY OF NEW ORLEANS MUSEUM OF ART ©

Best Art

New Orleans Museum of Art The city's premier art museum also serves as the centerpiece of City Park. (p110)

Ogden Museum of Southern Art Permanent and temporary exhibitions delve into the long creative legacy of the South. (p60)

Contemporary Arts Center A well-curated selection and packed events calendar make this an excellent outpost for discovering modern art. (p66)

Sydney & Walda Besthoff Sculpture Garden This peaceful venue allows visitors to peruse sculpture while enjoying the outdoors. (p110)

Best History

Cabildo The most comprehensive collection of material and artifacts related to Louisiana history. (p26)

The Historic New Orleans Collection Thoughtful exhibits explore selected vignettes from the city's past. (p32)

National WWII Museum A stunning exhibition space showcases tons of material related to the global conflict. (p58)

Presbytère Learn the story of Mardi Gras and the way public celebration is central to New Orleans' identity. (p33)

Gallier House Museum Take a stroll through centuries of fascinating

French Quarter architecture. (p33)

Best for Kids

Aquarium of the Americas Dive deep into an underwater world – mind the white gator! (p68)

Sydney & Walda Besthoff Sculpture Garden This outdoor exhibition has plenty of space for children to run around in. (p110)

New Orleans Museum of Art Admittedly a little hushed, but frequently hosts family-friendly events. (p110)

Backstreet Cultural Museum The colorful costumes and friendly docents make this museum unexpectedly family-friendly. (p120)

Best Theater

New Orleans has a strong theatrical bent; numerous local theater companies and a few large theatrical venues for touring productions frequently stage shows. The city has a long history of 'masking' – that is, finding any excuse to don a costume – and a love of embracing (and expressing) realms of dream and fantasy.

/GETTY IMAGES ©

New Movement Theater
(☎504-302-8264; www.newmovementtheater.com; 2706 St Claude Ave) Improv theater, by its nature, can be hit or miss. The best sort hits more than half the time; the New Movement, we can happily report, hits well above this average. The company has a cast of regular players from around the way and a stable schedule of classes that train new talent in the art of off-the-cuff comedy.

Old Marquer Theatre
(☎504-298-8676; www.oldmarquer.com; 2400 St Claude Ave) This small theater regularly features plays written and performed by local New Orleanians, as well as established shows from outside the city, plus events like poetry slams. There's an indie flavor to what's on offer, and the cozy atmosphere you get from witnessing a community of like-minded artists perform together.

Le Petit Théâtre du Vieux Carré (☎504-522-2081; www.lepetittheatre.com; 616 St Peter St) Going strong since 1916, Le Petit Théâtre is one of the oldest theater groups in the country. In its Jackson Sq home the troupe offers good repertory, with a proclivity for Southern dramas and special children's programming. Shows are sometimes followed by an informal cabaret performance, with the cast, audience and a resident ghost (so we hear) mingling over drinks.

Lupin Theatre (☎504-865-5106; Newcombe Circle, Dixon annex) The Lupin is the main performing arts center for Tulane University.

Survival Guide

Before You Go   148

When to Go 148
Book Your Stay 148

Arriving in New Orleans   149

Getting Around   150

Bicycle 150
Streetcar 150
Car 150
Taxi 150

Essential Information   151

Business Hours 151
Electricity 151
Money 151
Public Holidays 152
Safe Travel 152
Telephone 153
Travelers with Disabilities 153

Survival Guide

Before You Go

When to Go

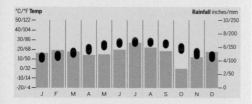

°C/°F Temp | Rainfall inches/mm

50/122 — — 10/250
40/104 — — 8/200
30/86 —
20/68 — — 6/150
10/50 — — 4/100
0/32 — — 2/50
-10/14 —
-20/-4 — — 0

J F M A M J J A S O N D

➜ **Jan–Mar** Carnival season! The weather is cool, parades are everywhere and Mardi Gras blows your mind.

➜ **Apr & May** Festival season! The weather is practically perfect and festivals kick off almost every weekend; expect high season rates.

➜ **Jun–Aug** Summer is hot and prone to hurricanes, but the crowds thin out.

➜ **Sep–Dec** Shoulder season. The city cools in October, and the events calendar continues at a low buzz.

Book Your Stay

The French Quarter offers historical properties, some with boutique design. The Central Business District (CBD) has similar lodgings, as well as larger, cheaper corporate hotels. Guesthouses and B&Bs can be found across the city. Book ahead, especially if a major festival occurs during your visit.

Useful Websites

New Orleans CVB (www. neworleanscvb.com/hotels) Comprehensive list of accommodations.

New Orleans Online (www.neworleansonline.com/ book) Hotel portal on the city's official tourism site.

Bed & Breakfast Inns of New Orleans (www.bbnola. com) Listings for B&Bs and guesthouses.

Lonely Planet (www. lonelyplanet.com) Author-recommended reviews and online booking.

Best Budget

Bywater Bed & Breakfast (www.bywaterbnb.com) Occupies the space between funky and cozy.

India House Hostel (www.indiahousehostel.com) Well-run hostel with a fun international clientele.

Lookout Inn of New Orleans (www.lookoutneworleans.com) Wonderfully weird outpost in the bohemian Bywater.

Prytania Park (www.prytaniaparkhotel.com) Reliably comfy and efficient budget option.

Best Midrange

Auld Sweet Olive Bed & Breakfast (www.sweetolive.com) Tropical decor infuses this wonderful Creole-cum-Victorian home.

La Belle Esplanade (www.labelleesplanade.com) Gorgeous historical home managed by an original New Orleans character.

Lafitte Guest House (www.lafitteguesthouse.com) Historical building that has been converted into a central, fun hotel.

Pierre Coulon Guest House (www.pierrecoulon guesthouse.com) Eclectic little cottage that balances quirk and warmth.

Best Top End

Audubon Cottages (www.auduboncottages.com) Gorgeous Creole suites located in the heart of the French Quarter.

Degas House (www.degashouse.com) Degas stayed at this Italianate home, as much a museum as it is accommodation.

Soniat House (www.soniathouse.com) One of the finest boutique properties in the French Quarter.

Park View Guest House (www.parkviewguesthouse.com) Fulfill those dreams of staying in an Uptown mansion.

Arriving in New Orleans

☑ **Top Tip** For the best way to get to your accommodation, see p17.

Louis Armstrong New Orleans International Airport

➡ Located 13 miles west of New Orleans.

➡ A taxi to the CBD costs $33, or $14 per passenger for three or more passengers.

➡ **Shuttles** (☎866-596-2699; www.airportshuttleneworleans.com) to the CBD cost $20/38 one-way/round-trip per person.

➡ The E-2 bus takes you to Carrollton and Tulane Ave in Mid-City for $2.

Greyhound & Amtrak Stations

➡ Adjacent to each other downtown at the **New Orleans Union Passenger Terminal** (☎504-299-1880, 1001 Loyola Ave).

➡ You can walk to the CBD or French Quarter, but don't do so at night, or with heavy luggage.

➡ A taxi from here to the French Quarter should cost around $10; further afield you'll be pressed to spend more than $20.

➡ The Loyola-UPT streetcar line runs to Canal St.

Getting Around

Bicycle

☑ **Best for**... Exploring neighborhoods and soaking up the city's atmosphere.

➡ New Orleans is pancake-flat and relatively compact. Our reviews are spread over an area roughly 8 miles wide.

➡ Heavy traffic, potholes, narrow roads and unsafe neighborhoods present some negatives to cycling.

➡ Fat tires are a near necessity.

➡ Beware of oppressive summer heat and humidity.

➡ All ferries offer free transportation for bicycles. Buses are now equipped with bike racks. Only folding bicycles are permitted on streetcars.

➡ Bicycles can be hired around town. We like **A Bicycle Named Desire** (Map p48, B1; ☎504-345-8966; www.abicyclenameddesire. com; 632 Elysian Fields Ave; 4/8/24hr rental $20/25/35, per additional day $25; ☺10am-5pm Wed-Mon) and **Bicycle Michael's** (Map p48, A1; ☎504-945-9505;

www.bicyclemichaels.com; 622 Frenchmen St; per day from $35; ☺10am-7pm Mon-Tue & Thu-Sat, to 5pm Sun).

Streetcar

☑ **Best for**... Casually exploring Uptown, the Garden District and parts of Mid-City.

➡ Four lines serve key routes in the city, run by the **Regional Transit Authority** (RTA; www.norta. com).

➡ Fares cost $1.25 – have exact change – or purchase a Jazzy Pass (one-/three-/31-day unlimited rides $3/9/55), which is also good on buses.

➡ Jazzy Passes can be purchased from streetcar conductors, from bus drivers, in Walgreens drugstores and from ticketing machines at RTA shelters along Canal St.

➡ Streetcars run about every 15 to 20 minutes, leaning towards every 30 minutes later at night, 24 hours a day.

Car

☑ **Best for**... Getting from one side of the city to the other.

➡ Having your own or renting a car can make it much easier to fully experience the city, from

Faubourg Marigny up to the Riverbend, and out along Esplanade Ave.

➡ If you are planning to spend most of your time in the French Quarter, don't bother with a car. You'll only end up wasting money on parking.

➡ Many city streets, even in posh Uptown, are in an atrocious state, and tires have accordingly short life spans.

➡ Be careful of left turns through intersections with a neutral ground (median), especially if a streetcar uses the neutral ground.

➡ Downtown on-street parking is typically for short-term use only.

➡ Parking enforcement officers are very vigilant in the French Quarter and CBD.

Taxi

☑ **Best for**... Traveling at night when alone or after a night's partying.

➡ **United Cabs** (☎504-522-9771; www.unitedcabs. com; ☺24hr) is the biggest and most reliable company in New Orleans.

➡ You might have to call for a pickup, unless you are in a central part of the French Quarter, where it is relatively easy to flag down a passing cab.

➔ Fares within the city start with a $3.50 flag-fall charge for one passenger (plus $1 for each additional passenger). From there it's $2 per mile. New Orleans is small, so don't expect fares to top $20.

Essential Information

Business Hours

New Orleans maintains business hours similar to much of the rest of the USA, except when it comes to bars.

Banks 9am to 5pm Monday to Thursday, 10am to 5:30pm Friday. Some branches are open 9am to noon Saturday.

Bars Usually 5pm until last customer leaves (official closing 2am on weekdays and 3am or 4am on weekends).

Post offices 8:30am to 4:30pm Monday to Friday and 8:30am to noon Saturday.

Restaurants 10am or 11am to 11pm (sometimes with a break from 2pm

to 5pm); usually closed Sunday and/or Monday.

Stores 10am to 7pm or 8pm.

Electricity

The electrical current in the USA is 110V to 115V, 60Hz AC. Outlets may be suited to flat two-prong (not grounded) or three-prong (grounded) plugs. If your appliance is made for another electrical system, you will need a transformer or adaptor; if you didn't bring one along, buy one at any consumer electronics store around town.

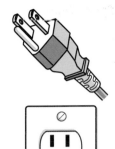

120V/60Hz

120V/60Hz

Money

There are three straightforward ways to handle money in the USA: cash; US-dollar traveler's checks; and credit or bank cards, which can be used to withdraw cash from the many automatic teller machines (ATMs) across the country. US dollars are the only accepted currency in New Orleans.

ATMs

With a Visa card, MasterCard or bank card affiliated with the Plus or Cirrus networks, you can easily obtain cash from ATMs all over the city.

Changing Money

Most major currencies and leading brands of traveler's checks are easily exchanged in New Orleans. You will also find various independent exchange bureaus.

When you first arrive at the airport, you can change money at **Travel-Ex America Business Center** on the 2nd floor of the West Terminal. **TravelEx** charges a sliding service fee. The **Western Union** section of the office closes at 4:30pm Monday through Friday and 2:30pm Saturday and Sunday.

Whitney National Bank on the 2nd floor of the West Terminal also changes money, charging a flat $15 service fee if you don't have an account with them.

Better exchange rates are generally available at banks in the CBD. The main office of Whitney National Bank buys and sells foreign currency.

Credit & Debit Cards

Major credit cards are widely accepted by car-rental agencies and most hotels, restaurants, gas stations, shops and larger grocery stores. Many smaller restaurants and bars accept cash only. The most commonly accepted cards are Visa, MasterCard and American Express. Discover and Diners Club cards are also accepted by a large number of businesses.

Public Holidays

Note that when national holidays fall on a weekend, they are often celebrated on the nearest Friday or Monday, so that everyone enjoys a three-day weekend. **Mardi Gras**, which does not have a fixed date, is an official holiday in New Orleans; to see future dates, visit www.mardi-grasneworleans.com.

The following are all national holidays:

New Year's Day January 1

Martin Luther King Jr Day Third Monday in January

Presidents' Day Third Monday in February

Memorial Day Last Monday in May

Independence Day July 4

Labor Day First Monday in September

Columbus Day Second Monday in October

Veterans Day November 11

Thanksgiving Fourth Thursday in November

Christmas Day December 25

Safe Travel

New Orleans has an atrocious crime rate. The vast majority of violent crime occurs between parties who already know each

Money-Saving Tips

➜ Many bars offer free red beans and rice on Monday nights.

➜ Parks such as Audubon (p92), City Park (p106) and the Besthoff Sculpture Garden (p110) have free admission.

➜ High-end restaurants usually have midrange lunch specials.

➜ A Second Line (p123) parade and similar events are like free mobile concerts.

other, but tourists are occasionally targeted.

Exercise the caution you would in any US city. The possibility of getting mugged is something to consider even in areas you'd think are safe (eg the Garden District). Solo pedestrians are targeted more often than people walking in groups, and daytime is a better time to be out on foot than nighttime.

If your hotel or vehicle is situated on the margins of the French Quarter, you might want to take a taxi back at night. The CBD and Warehouse District have plenty of activity during weekdays, but they're relatively deserted at night and on weekends. B&Bs along Esplanade Ridge are close enough to troubled neighborhoods to call for caution at night.

Pedestrians crossing the street do not have the right of way and motorists (unless they are from out of state) will not yield. Whether on foot or in a car, be wary before entering an intersection, as New Orleans drivers are notorious for running yellow and even red lights.

To see where crime is occurring before you visit, log on to www.crimemapping.com/map/la/neworleans.

Telephone

The area code in New Orleans is ☏504. In Thibodaux and Houma it's ☏985; Baton Rouge and surrounds ☏225; and Shreveport and the northern part of the state ☏318.

When dialing a number with a different area code from your own, you must dial ☏1 before the area code. For example, to call a Baton Rouge number from New Orleans, begin by dialing ☏1-225. Note that hotel telephones often have heavy surcharges.

Travelers with Disabilities

New Orleans is somewhat lax in catering to people with disabilities.

Sidewalk curbs rarely have ramps, and many historic public buildings and hotels are not equipped to meet the needs of wheelchair-users. Modern hotels adhere to standards established by the federal Americans with Disabilities Act by providing ramps, elevators and accessible bathrooms.

Red streetcars on the Canal St, Riverfront and Loyola-UPT streetcar lines are accessible to disabled riders. The green streetcars that run along St Charles Ave are protected from changes by the National Register of Historic Places and have not been made accessible (see www.norta.com/accessibility.aspx). Regional Transit Authority buses offer a lift service; for information about paratransit service (alternative transportation for those who can't ride regular buses), call **RTA Paratransit** (☏ queries 504-827-8345, scheduling 504-827-7433; www.norta.com).

Behind the Scenes

Send Us Your Feedback

We love to hear from travelers – your comments help make our books better. We read every word, and we guarantee that your feedback goes straight to the authors. Visit **lonelyplanet.com/contact** to submit your updates and suggestions.

Note: We may edit, reproduce and incorporate your comments in Lonely Planet products such as guidebooks, websites and digital products, so let us know if you don't want your comments reproduced or your name acknowledged. For a copy of our privacy policy visit lonelyplanet.com/privacy.

Adam's Thanks

Thank you: the Bobellershaws (Mike and Nora), whose generosity of spirit is a model for this entire city, if not the world; Andrew Holbein the Jazzman and Zach the Younger-Man, who both pushed me so hard to be here; Dan Favre and Trish Kelly, for general winning all over the place; and just too many New Orleans people to mention – an extended family that has encompassed and embraced my actual family: AJ, Halle, Matt, Maria, Adrian, Darcy, Molly, Travis, Kate, Paige, Morgan, David, Jonah, Melissa, Rob, Katie, Carin...the list goes on. Thank you Amy Balfour for hanging like a champ; Dora Whitaker for putting me on this passion project of a book; mom and dad for letting me live here with their blessings; Gizmo, for warming my lap as I write; and most of all Rachel, for her enormous love and support, and my Sanda, whose fresh eyes see the city better than all of us.

Acknowledgments

Cover photograph: St Louis Cathedral, Jackson Square, French Quarter, New Orleans, Werner Bertsch/4Corners.

This Book

This 2nd edition of *Pocket New Orleans* was coordinated by Adam Karlin and written and researched by Adam Karlin and Amy C Balfour. This guidebook was produced by the following:

Destination Editor Dora Whitaker **Product Editors** Katie O'Connell, Martine Power **Senior Cartographer** Alison Lyall **Book Designer** Jessica Rose **Assisting Editors** Susan Paterson, Gabrielle Stefanos **Cover Researcher** Campbell McKenzie

Thanks to Sasha Baskett, Sarah Billington, Hilary Charlesworth, Blake Haney, Anna Keaschuk, Kate Kiely, Kathleen Leonore, Kate Mathews, Diana Saengkham, Dianne Schallmeiner, Eleanor Simpson, Lyahna Spencer, John Taufa

Index

A

accommodations 148-9
African American culture 122
air travel 17, 149
airports 149
Alcee Fortier Park 110, 112
Alex Beard Studio 63
American Photo Safari 142
Aquarium of the Americas 68
architecture 140-1
area codes 153
Ariodante 63
art galleries 62-3, see also museums
Arthur Roger Gallery 63
Ashé Cultural Arts Center 81
ATMs 151
Audubon, see Uptown & Audubon
Audubon Park 92-3
Audubon Park Golf Course 93
Audubon Zoological Gardens 11, 90-1

Sights 000
Map Pages **000**

B

Backstreet Cultural Museum 120
Backstreet culture 122
bars 137, see also Drinking subindex
Bayou St John 110, see also Mid-City & Bayou St John
Beard, Alex 63
Beauregard-Keyes House 34, 129
beignets 39
bicycle travel, see cycling
Botanical Gardens 107
brass bands 135
Brevard House 131
bus travel 17
business hours 151
Bywater, see Faubourg Marigny & Bywater

C

Cabildo 9, 26-7
car travel 150
Carousel Gardens 107
CBD & Warehouse District 56-71, **64-5**
drinking 69-71
entertainment 71
food 66-9
itineraries 57, 62-3
shopping 71
sights 58-61, 66
transportation 57
cell phones 16
changing money 152
children, travel with 139
City Park 11, 106-7
climate 148
Clouet Gardens 52
clubs 137
Confederacy of Cruisers 142
Congo Square 124
Contemporary Arts Center 66
cooking courses 82
costs 16, 152
credit cards 152
Creole heritage 35
Crescent Park 49
culture 122
currency 16
cycling 51, 150

D

dangers 152-3
debit cards 152
disabilities, travelers with 153
drinking, see Drinking subindex, individual neighborhoods
driving 150

E

electricity 16, 151
entertainment, see Entertainment subindex, individual neighborhoods
Esplanade Avenue 123
events, see festivals

F

Faubourg Marigny & Bywater 44-55, **46, 48**
drinking 52
entertainment 53-4
food 50-2
itineraries 45, 46-7
shopping 54-5
sights 49-50
transportation 45
Faulkner, William 43
festivals 143
Fly, the 93
food 132-3, see also Eating subindex, individual neighborhoods
French Market 32
French Quarter 22-43, **30-1**
drinking 39-42
entertainment 42-3
food 36-9
itineraries 23

French Quarter
continued
shopping 43
sights 24-9, 32-4
transportation 23
French Quarter Festival 143
Frenchmen Art Market 50
Frenchmen Street 49
Freret Street 98
Friends of the Cabildo 142

G
galleries 62-3, *see also* museums
Gallier House Museum 33-4, 129
Garden & Lower Garden Districts 72-85, **78-9**
drinking 84
entertainment 84
food 81-3
itineraries 73, 76-7
shopping 84-5
sights 74-5, 80-1, 83
transportation 73
gardens 144
Gay Pride New Orleans 143
gay travelers 138
George Schmidt Gallery 63
golf 93
Goodrich-Stanley House 130
Grace King House 130

H
Higgins, Andrew 66
highlights 8-11, 12-13
Historic New Orleans Collection 32
history 35, 36, 50, 110, 111, 124, 145
Hogan Jazz Archive 93
holidays 152
House of Broel 83, 130-1
Hurricane Katrina 111

I
internet resources 16, 148-9
Irish Channel 80
itineraries 14-15, 128-31, *see also individual neighborhoods*

J
Jackson Square 8, 28-9
Jackson Statue 29
Jazz Fest 143
jazz music 135
Jean Bragg Gallery of Southern Art 62

L
Lafayette Cemetery No 1 10, 74-5, 80
Le Musée de f.p.c. **121, 123**
Lemieux Galleries 63
lesbian travelers 138
live music 134-5
local life 12-13
Louis Armstrong Park 120-1
Lower Garden District, *see* Garden & Lower Garden Districts

M
Magazine Street 76-7
Mardi Gras 97, 143
Mardi Gras Indians 120
Mardi Gras World 69
McGehee School for Girls 131
McKenna Museum of African American Art 80
Mid-City & Bayou St John 104-15, **108-9**
drinking 113-14
entertainment 114-15
food 112-13
itineraries 105
shopping 115
sights 106-7, 110, 112
transportation 105
Milton Latter Memorial Library 96
Mississippi River 34
mobile phones 16
money 16, 151-2
muffuletta 40
museums 145
music 134-5

N
National WWII Museum 10, 58-9, 66
Native American culture 120
New Orleans African American Museum 121
New Orleans Arts District Arts Walk 143
New Orleans Culinary History Tours 142
New Orleans Museum of Art 110

Newcomb Art Gallery 93
nightlife 134-5

O
Ogden Museum of Southern Art 10, 60-1
Old US Mint 32-3
opening hours 151

P
parking 70
parks 144
Pedicabs 32
Pitot House 110
Plessy v Ferguson Plaque 50
Pontalba Buildings 29
Presbytère 33
Preservation Resource Center 66
public holidays 152

R
REpurposingNOLA Piece by Peace 63
Rice, Anne 80, 131
Riverbend 102
drinking 103
food 103
shopping 103
transportation 102
Riverfront 32
Roger, Arthur 63
Royal Street 9, 24-5

S
safe travel 152-3
Schmidt, George 63
Second Lines 122
self-catering 38
shopping 76-7, 136, *see also* Shopping subindex, *individual neighborhoods*

Soren Christensen Gallery 63

Soul of Nola 142

Southern Food & Beverage Museum 82

St Augustine's Church 120

St Charles Avenue Streetcar 11, 88-9

St Claude Square 47

St Joseph's Day – Super Sunday 143

St Louis Cathedral 29

St Patrick's Day 143

Storyland 107

streetcars 11, 88-9, 150

Sydney & Walda Besthoff Sculpture Garden 110

....

T

taxis 150-1

telephone services 16, 153

Tennessee Williams Literary Festival 143

theater 146

The Fly 93

time 16

tipping 16

top sights 8-11

tours 142

Tours by Judy 142

transportation 17, 149-51

Tremé 116-25, **118-19**

  entertainment 124-5

  food 123-4

  itineraries 117

  sights 120-3

  transportation 117

Tulane University 93

....

U

Uptown & Audubon 86-101, **94**

  drinking 99-100

  entertainment 100

  food 96, 98-9

  itineraries 87, 92-3

  shopping 101

  sights 88-91, 96

  transportation 87

Ursuline Convent 34, 129

Ursuline nuns 36

USS Tang 59

....

V

vacations 152

visas 16

voodoo 122

....

W

walking tours 142

  A Night of Jazz & Live Music 46-7, **46**

  Audubon Park 92-3, **92**

  Balconies & Courtyards 128-9, **129**

  Exploring the Riverbend 102-3, **102**

  Gallery-Hopping in the Arts District 62-3, **62**

  Garden District Stroll 130-1, **131**

  Shopping on Magazine Street 76-7, **76**

Walter Grinnan Robinson House 131

Warehouse District, see CBD & Warehouse District

weather 148

websites 16, 148-9

Williams, Tennessee 54, 143

....

Z

zoo 11, 90-1

zydeco music 134, 135

....

⊗ Eating

....

A

American Sector 59

Angelo Brocato 112

Avenue Pub 130

....

B

Ba Chi Canteen 103

Bacchanal 50

Bayona 36

....

C

Café Beignet 39

Café Degas 112

Café du Monde 39

Café Reconcile 83

Cake Café & Bakery 51-2

Camellia Grill 103

Carmo 69

Central Grocery 40

Clancy's 96

Cochon 67-8

Cochon Butcher 68

Commander's Palace 82

Coop's Place 36

Cooter Brown's 103

Coquette 82

Croissant D'Or Patisserie 37

....

D

Dat Dog 98

Delachaise 98

District: Donuts Sliders Brew 77

Domenica 68-9

Domilise's Po-Boys 98

Dragon's Den 46

....

E

Elizabeth's 51

....

G

Gautreau's 96

Green Goddess 39

Guy's 98

....

H

Herbsaint 68

....

J

Joint 51

Juan's Flying Burrito 83

....

L

Liuzza's by the Track 112

Luke 68

....

M

Mahony's Po-Boy Shop 96

Mandina's 113

Maurepas Foods 51

Mister Gregory's 38

Mona Lisa 38

Morning Call 107

....

P

Pagoda Cafe 112-13

Parasol's 82-3

Parkway Tavern 112

Patois 98-9

Peche Seafood Grill 66-7

Pizza Delicious 50-1

Port of Call 37

Preservation Hall 42

R

Red's Chinese 50
Restaurant August 67
Ruby Slipper –
  Downtown 69

S

Seoul Shack 46
Slice 83
SoBou 36-7
Stein's Deli 82
Surrey's Juice Bar 81
Sylvain 38

T

Tan Dinh 133
Toup's Meatery 113

V

Verti Marte 38

🍷 Drinking

Avenue Pub 84
Bellocq 70
BJ's 52
Boot 99
Bourbon Pub & Parade 42
Bulldog 84
Cane & Table 40
Capdeville 70
Chart Room 40
Circle Bar 69
Columns Hotel 100
Cosimo's 40
Country Club 52
Cure 99

Erin Rose 40
Fair Grinds 113
Finn McCool's 114
French 75 40-1
Freret Street Publiq
  House 99
Gene's 47
Half Moon 76
Lafitte's Blacksmith
  Shop 41
Latitude 29 39
Le Bon Temps Roulé
  100
Lost Love 52
Lucy's Retired Surfers
  Bar 70-1
Maison 47
Maple Leaf Bar 103
Mid-City Yacht Club
  114
Mimi's in the Marigny
  52
Molly's at the
  Market 39
NOLA Brewing 84
Oz 42
Pal's 114
Phoenix 47
Rusty Nail 70
Saint Bar & Lounge 84
Spitfire Coffee 41
St Joe's 99
Tonique 39
Treo 113
Twelve Mile Limit 113
Yuki 47

😊 Entertainment

AllWays Lounge 53
Café Negril 47
Candlelight Lounge
  124
Chickie Wah Wah
  114-15
d.b.a. 53-4
Gasa Gasa 100
Hi Ho Lounge 54
House of Blues 42-3
Howlin' Wolf 71
K-Doe's Mother-in-Law
  Lounge 124
Le Petit Théâtre du
  Vieux Carré 146
Lupin Theatre 146
Mahalia Jackson
  Theater 124
Marigny Opera House
  53
Mid-City Rock & Bowl
  114
New Movement Theater
  146
Old Marquer Theatre
  146
Palm Court Jazz
  Café 42
Prytania Theatre 100-1
Republic New Orleans
  71
Saenger Theatre 125
Snug Harbor 54
Spotted Cat 54
Tipitina's 100
Zeitgeist 84

🛍 Shopping

Aidan Gill 77
Bywater Bargain
  Center 55
Chiwawa Gaga 43
Crescent City
  Comics 101
Esoterica Occult
  Goods 43
Euclid Records 55
Faubourg Marigny Book
  Store 55
Faulkner House Books
  43
Fifi Mahony's 43
Funky Monkey 84-5
GoGo Jewelry 77
Green Eyed Gator 43
Green Project 140
I.J. Reilly's 54-5
Jim Russell Records 77
Louisiana Music
  Factory 55
Magazine Antique
  Mall 85
Maple Street Book
  Shop 103
Meyer the Hatter 71
New Orleans Music
  Exchange 77
Simon of New Orleans
  77
SoPo 115
Storyville 77
Trashy Diva 85
Tubby & Coos 115
Uptown Costume &
  Dancewear 101
Yvonne La Fleur 103

Sights 000
Map Pages **000**

Our Writers

Adam Karlin

Adam lives in New Orleans with his wife, daughter, dog and lizard. He has written more than 45 guidebooks for Lonely Planet, primarily covering the Americas, but stretching as far afield as the Andaman Islands to the Zimbabwe border (get it? A–Z? Never mind).

Contributing Writer

Amy C Balfour contributed to the CBD & Warehouse District, Garden & Lower Garden Districts, Uptown & Audubon, Mid-City & Bayou St John and Tremé content.

Published by Lonely Planet Publications Pty Ltd
ABN 36 005 607 983
2nd edition – Nov 2015
ISBN 978 1 74179 935 4
© Lonely Planet 2015   Photographs © as indicated 2015
10 9 8 7 6 5 4 3 2 1
Printed in China